DASARA DISCOURSES 1998

By
Bhagavaan Shri Sathya Sai Baba
(delivered from 25th Sept to 1st Oct 1998)

Prashaanthi Nilayam

Sri Sathya Sai Books and Publications Trust

Prashaanthi Nilayam PO 515 134
Anantapur District, Andhra Pradesh, India
Gram: "BOOK TRUST" - Phone: 87375, 87236
Fax: 91-8555 - 87236 & 87390 STD Code: 08555
ISD Code: 00-91-8555

International Standard Book Number - 81-7208-264-9

Published by:

The Convener, Sri Sathya Sai Books and Publications Trust,
Prashaanthi Nilayam, India - Pin Code 515 134
Phone: 87375 / 87236, STD:08555 ISD: 91-08555
FAX: 91-8555-87236 and 87390

First Edition : Nov. 1998
Second Edition : May 1999

Price Rs.20.00

Printed at:
          PRINT PARK,
          284, I Main, 407, S.F.S.,
          Yelahanka New Town,
          BANGALORE-560 065
          Phone:080-846 0784

Contents

Pages

INTRODUCTION

Bhagavaan Shri Sathya Sai Baba has been conducting for many years since 1961, a Seven Day Vedha Purusha Jnaana Yagna, a Vedhik Fire-Sacrifice at Prashaanthi Nilayam. Such a Yagna has been performed from 25th September to 1st October 1998 in Puurna Chandhra Auditorium.

Yagna is the means for securing awareness of the Divine and peace and happiness in society. It may be asked why the Yagna is performed for seven days. The number seven has a special significance in the divine creation. For instance, there are said to be seven worlds, seven sages, seven seas, seven sacred mountains, seven colours of the Sun's ray and seven notes of music and so on. If these are worshipped as symbols of the Divine, awareness of the Divine arises. By the performance of the Yagna for seven days according to the Vedhik injunctions, man can acquire the ability to get rid of the seven veils of ignorance, ascend the seven stages of spiritual knowledge and achieve liberation.

This Yagna begins with the lighting of the sacred sacrificial fire by the rigid rubbing of two sacred wooden sticks, symbolic of the latent presence of the Divine in every object of creation.

In this Yagna seven principal deities or divine potencies are worshipped: Ganesha (Remover of obstacles), Suurya (the energising Sun God), Dhevi (the Divine Mother), Brahma (the Propagator of the Vedhas), Vishnu (all persasive Divinity), Shiva (the Great God of Auspiciousness) and Agni (the Fire God). Bhagavaan declares that all these divine potencies are in man.

The central aspect of this Yagna is the offerings to Shiva in the sacrificial fireplace on all the seven days of the Yagna with the chanting of the sacred hymn, 'Rudhram'. On the final day of this Yagna, Bhagavaan materialises various precious objects and offers them to the sacrificial fire. Bhagavaan has declared that what everyone should offer in the sacrificial fire are his bad qualities. Bhagavaan has also explained that the sacred smoke rising from the sacrificial fire, fully charged with the power of the sacred Vedhik manthras enters the clouds and purifies the rain-water and it also purifies the pollution in the atmosphere.

This Yagna is marked by the clear chanting of the Vedhas. The Vedhas are eternal and are the basis for all Dharma. Bhaarath is esteemed as the soul of the Vedhas, whose glory is repeatedly declared by Bhagavaan in His many discourses.

Bhagavaan's discourses during the seven days of the Yagna are veritable feasts for the thousands of devotees from here and abroad. Bhagavaan explains in the simplest language profoundest Vedhaanthik Truths; in these discourses. Bhagavaan conveys forcefully the message of the Adhvaithik wisdom of the oneness of the individual self and the Supreme Self. This indeed is the real purpose of this Jnaana Yagna.

OM SHRI SAI RAAM

QUEST FOR TRUTH

(Divine Discourse on 25.9.1998)

Sathyam Maathaa, Pithaa Jnaanam,
Dharmo Bhraatha, Dhaya Sakhaa,
Shaantham Pathnee, Kshamaa Puthraha,
Shadethe Nija Baandhavaah

Embodiments of Love!

"Sathyam Maathaah": In this world, every individual has a mother. But Truth is the mother of the entire humanity. Those who follow this mother will never face any difficulties in life. The worldly mothers are bound by space and time and will have to leave their bodies at one point of time, but Truth is not limited by space and time and remains the same in all the three periods of time. It is the master of all the three worlds. So, everyone must necessarily follow such a noble mother of Truth.

KNOW YOUR TRUE RELATIONS

"Pithaa Jnaanam": Wisdom is the father. Wisdom does not mean worldly knowledge. *"Advaitha Dharshanam Jnaanam"*, True Wisdom confers the experience of non - dualism.

"Dharmo Bhraathaa": Dharma is the brother. This brother is the embodiment of Love, and loves the entire humanity, irrespective of caste, creed, nationality and religion. Basing on this, the Vedhas gave utmost importance to Truth and Righteousness. In the great epic Raamaayana, Lakshmana personified this principle of Dharma. When he fainted in the battlefield, Raama lamented saying that he could get a consort like Seetha, a mother like Kausalya, but not a brother like Lakshmana. Raama said His Divinity blossomed because He had a brother like Lakshmana.

"Dhayaa Sakhaa": Compassion is the true friend. In this world a friend today may become an enemy tomorrow. But, there is no greater friend than Compassion.

"Shaantham Pathnee": Peace is the wife. This is the precious jewel of saints, and is the royal path in the spiritual field.

"Kshamaa Puthraha": Forgiveness is the son. There is no greater quality than forgiveness. It encompasses all the good qualities like Truth, Righteousness, Non-violence and it is the essence of all Vedhas.

Therefore, for every individual the true relations are Truth, Wisdom, Righteousness, Compassion, Peace and Forgiveness. The whole world is full of agitation and disturbance because of lack of these sacred qualities.

DIVINE MOTHER - EMBODIMENT OF TRUTH

Embodiments of Love!

You should always remember your true mother and father. You cannot exist without them. The whole creation has emerged from Truth and merges back into it. There is no place where Truth does not exist. It is the good fortune of human beings to have this eternal Truth as their mother. But, today humanity does not follow such a sacred mother. You worship Goddess Dhevi in these nine days, *Dhevi Navaraathri.* You consider Dhevi as your Divine Mother. This Dhevi (Divine Mother) is called *Sathya Svaruupini,* which means She is the embodiment of Truth. So, worshipping Truth amounts to worshipping the Divine Mother, Dhevi. If you understand and follow this truth, you will be successful in every field. The Vedhas also proclaim this Truth. There are many in this world who have gone through the Vedhas and the sacred texts, but their views seem to be distorted, perverted. Since ancient times, the sages and saints undetook many spiritual practices in their quest for Truth. They were determined not to give up till they had the vision of Truth. Ultimately, they declared to the world that they had seen God, who is all brilliance, full of effulgence and is beyond the darkness of ignorance. They also declared that God is not present in a distant land, but is in the human body. The saints had the vision of God, who is *Chinmaya* (full of Awareness) in the body, which is *Mrinmaya* (made of clay). So, we should not underrate the human body and use it for mean and worldly pleasures. Body is the temple of God. This body may be compared to an iron chest. Just as the precious jewels are kept in the iron chest, so also God is present in the human body. So, the body has to be maintained and made proper use of for the sake of the precious jewel, Atma. You get jewels only from earth. Similarly, you have to search for the jewel of the Aathma in the body itself, which is made of clay.

SHED EGO AND ATTACHMENT

Let us investigate, what comes in the way of experiencing the Aathmic Principle. Ego and attachment stand as obstacles in our path. Only when you give up this ego and attachment, you will have purity of heart, which in turn will lead to the experience of Supreme Wisdom. The more you develop attachment, the more restless you become. Ego is much more dangerous. It has become an incurable disease in human beings. So, you have to keep the ego and attachment under control and engage yourself in the quest of Aathmik bliss.

MATTER AND ENERGY ARE INSEPARABLE

During these sacred nine days *(Navaraathri),* people go through the sacred texts such as Dhevi Bhaagavatha, Raamaayana and Mahaabhaaratha. People also worship the deities Dhurga, Lakshmi and Sarasvathi. This Trinity is present in the principle of Truth. Goddess Gaayathri has three aspects. They are: Gaayathri, Saavithri and Sarasvathi. Gaayathri is the presiding deity of your senses. Saavithri is the presiding deity of the Life Principle. Sarasvathi is the presiding deity of speech. All these three are within the same principle of Truth. Gaayathri Manthra begins with *"Om Bhur Bhuvah Suvah"*. *'Bhur'* means Materialisation (body); *'Bhuvah'* means Vibration (Life Principle); *'Suvah'* means Radiation (Aathma). Venkataraman, the previous speaker said that the matter became energy and vice versa. From a scientist's point of view, that is true. But, in My view, matter and energy do not exist separately. Matter is energy and energy is matter. These two are inseparable and interrelated. In fact, there is no matter in this world, wherever you see, you find only energy.

During these nine days Goddess Shakthi (Principle of Energy) is worshipped. Truth, Righteousness, Peace, Forgiveness are all the expressions of the Principle of Shakthi. Truth is the primal cause. There is nothing other than this. All faculties of energy are present in this

Truth. So consider Truth as your mother and follow it. The Vedhas proclaim, *"Sathyam Vadha; Dharmam Chara"*, which means speak the Truth and follow Righteousness. Unfortunately, today people do not follow this. This is the cause of all suffering. Ancients gave utmost priority to Truth and Righteousness. They followed the dictates of their conscience. But today such an attitude is lacking.

WHAT IS QUEST FOR TRUTH?

Many people say they are in search of Divinity. Once you follow the path of Truth, you will find Divinity everywhere. A small example: The same eyes see the mother, daughter, wife and sister. Here you need to enquire as to what kind of feeling you should have towards each. This is the quest for Truth. Mother should be viewed with reverence and respect, daughter should be considered as a part of your own being. In this way you should enquire and understand the Truth.

If you just go by the direct evidence of what you see, you will never know the Truth. All that you see is bound to perish. There are many things, which cannot be perceived by the naked eye. In the spiritual path everyone wants direct evidence *(Pratyaksha Pramana)*. But direct evidence cannot constitute the entire Truth. For example: You see a person who is four feet five inches tall, weighing forty-five kilograms and fair complexioned. All these can be seen by the naked eye. But you cannot go merely by these physical qualities. You should also take into consideration the unseen qualities in him such as love, compassion, anger etc. It is utter foolishness if you go by the physical form, which is direct evidence. It is not possible to see the direct manifestation of God. God, who is the embodiment of Truth and Righteousness, is everywhere. So, you practise Truth and Righteousness and enjoy the bliss.

TURN YOUR VISION INWARD

For everything, conscience is the witness. If you do not follow the conscience, everything becomes unsacred. Atma is the eternal witness and that is conscience. Atma is everywhere. It is attributeless, every individual and every creature. It has no form. It is attributeless, eternal, ancient, unsullied, immortal. Who can understand such an Aathmik Principle? You speak of Truth and consider whatever you see and hear as Truth, but all this is limited to senses. But Aathma (the true Self) is beyond the senses. Then how to know this Aathmik Principle? You do not need to search for this elsewhere. Turn your vision inward. The Vedhas said: *"Pashyannapi na pashyathi muudho"*, he is a fool who sees, yet does not see. All that you see is Divine, but you mistake it for Nature. The one with Aathmik vision will see the entire Nature as Divine. But if you have the worldly view, you can only see the world. *"Vishvam Vishnumayam,"* Vishnu pervades the entire universe. Names and forms may vary, but Aathma is uniform in all. To understand this unity, you have to turn your vision inward. There is no separate path to know God other than knowing one's own Self.

There is no human being that has no hunger for food. Similarly, you should also have hunger for God. Some people may call it madness; that is their madness. Each has his faith, conviction and experience. No one has the right to criticise others.

AATHMA HAS NO BIRTH OR DEATH

It is only the body that has birth and death, but Atma has no birth and no death. It has no beginning and no end. It is the all pervading eternal Brahma. Who is Brahma? He is not the one with four heads as described in books. Brahma is vastness. You find only Brahma wherever you see. This expansion of Love is God. The feeling of 'my body' is contraction of Love, which is death. So, you should expand your Love. Your Love should not be limited to your family and relations.

In Mathematics $1+1+1+1$ becomes 4. The number increases or decreases depending on whether 1 is added or subtracted. But in spiritual mathematics, Aathma+Aathma+Aathma results again in Aathma. It does not increase or decrease. The first name of Aathma is 'I'. Vedhas declared: *"Aham Brahmasmi"* (I am Brahman). This 'I' is the first name of God. It is possible to know this 'I' only by following the path of Truth.

MISTAKE LIES IN VISION, NOT IN CREATION

In this World, only Truth exists, there is no falsehood. If you find falsehood, the mistake lies in your *Drishti,* (vision) and not in the *Srishti* (creation). If you put on blue glasses, the world appears as blue in colour; if you put on red glasses, you will find only redness all around. The defect lies with the colour of the glasses, but not with the world. The very principle of creation is Divinity. *"Sarvam Khalvidham Brahma",* so revere everyone as Brahma. Love everyone as Brahma. Then there will be no scope for hatred or enmity. What is the reason for all agitation in this world? It is the lack of equanimity. Only through equanimity, you can develop Love.

Embodiments of Love!

In these seven days of Yajna, we have seven modes of worship. We call it *Sapthaha,* seven - day event. What is the significance of having a *'Sapthaha'?* This number 'Seven' is very significant in Numerology. In music, we have Saptha Svaras (seven notes). There are Seven Oceans,

Seven Rishis, Seven Colours and Seven Worlds. They are all within us. There is nothing beyond you. It is foolishness to think that God is separate from you and search for Him outside. You are God. But since you identify yourself with body, you are not able to understand this Truth. Body is like a water bubble, and mind is like a mad monkey. Why do you rely on these two? Follow your conscience. Only then you will have self-satisfaction.

FOSTER SACRED QUALITIES

Aathma symbolises 'Hridhaya' (Spiritual Heart). God dwells in 'Hridhaya'. Only sacred qualities should emerge out of 'Hridhaya'. 'Hridhaya' is the centre of Love and Peace. But instead, animal qualities like anger, hatred and jealousy emerge; then you are a beast, not a human being. Such a heart is a dwelling place for animals, not God. If you conduct yourself with peace, love and compassion, then you are God. The Navaraathri worship has been started to foster sacred qualities in us. Dhurga, Lakshmi and Sarasvathi symbolise the three attributes, Sathva, Rajas and Thamas.

You would have heard the name of 'Dhasharatha'. Who is he? He is not the king of Ayodhya. Dhasharatha refers to the human body that has five senses of perception and five senses of action. The master of these ten senses is Dhasharatha.

This body is a chariot and Dhasharatha is the master of this Chariot. He has three wives. They signify Saathvik, Raajasik and Thaamasik qualities. He has four sons. They signify the four objectives of life: Dharma, Artha, Kaama and Moksha. (Righteousness, Wealth, Desire, Fulfilment and Liberation) What is the capital of Dhasaratha's Kingdom? 'Ayodhya', which means it is a place where no one can get into. It signifies 'Hridhaya', where no wicked qualities can enter.

YOUR OWN ACTIONS CAUSE HEAVEN OR HELL

The entire universe is within you. The mountains may appear smooth from a distance, but once you go near, you will know the truth. It is the distance that lends enchantment. As long as you think that Kailasa, Vaikuntha and Svarga are at a distant place, you will go crazy thinking of them. But actually all of them are in your 'Hridhaya'. Your happiness is heaven and your misery is hell. The concept of hell and heaven has been introduced in order to see that you do only good. Heaven and hell are not separate; they are in your mind. What is the cause of misery? Your own actions.

Buddha did penance for six long years. One day he opened his eyes and said, he had caught hold of the thief. Who is the thief? It is the mind. He realised that mind was the root cause of all suffering. If you control your mind, you will never suffer. Churchill said, "Man has conquered everything, but he has not conquered himself". Man is trying to know everything without understanding his true Self. Know Thyself, then you will know everything. This is what the Upanishaths said, "Try to know and experience that by which everything is known and experienced." That is Aaathmik bliss which is eternal and supreme. *"True happiness lies in union with God."* If you are with the world, you will never get happiness.

WORSHIP GOD AS YOUR MOTHER

Human heart can be compared to the Ocean of Milk *(Ksheera Saagara)*, but today it has become one of salinity *(Kshaara Saagara)*. Lord Vishnu dwells on the Ocean of Milk, which means He resides in our hearts. But if we make our heart into *'Kshaara Saagara'*, then whales and sharks (bad qualities) enter. Human heart should be pure, only then Lord Vishnu can reside in it. If you understand God, you will not search for Him outside. *"God is with you, in you, above you, below you, around you"*. There is no one nearer than God. God is nearer than your physical mother. So, worship God as your mother, who is the embodiment of Truth.

I always begin My discourse with a Shloka or a poem and conclude it with a Bhajan. Do you know what they are? The first poem or

Shloka is like a plate, the discourse can be compared to the various delicious items that are served on the plate, and the Bhajan in the end is like a plate covering the delicious items. Do not treat this as a *Mandhu* (medicine), thereby taking a little of it. Treat this as a *Vindhu* (banquet) and partake of the delicious items that I serve to the maximum extent. Experience and enjoy this banquet.

Students! Embodiments of Love!

You have to learn many things in daily life. First know the mistakes in your life and try to correct them. Love is essential to become a complete human being. If you follow the path of Love, everything becomes Love.

(Bhagavaan concluded His discourse with the Bhajan, *"Prema mudhitha manase kaho..."*)

(Speak with a love filled heart)

❋ ❋ ❋

GOD, THE ONLY REFUGE

(Divine Discourse on 26.9.1998)

One may master all knowledge and
vanquish one's adversaries in argumentation
One may be mighty to fight with valour and courage in the battlefield
One may be an emperor reigning over vast kingdoms
One may offer cows and gold as an act of charity
One may count the countless stars in the sky
One may tell the names of different living creatures on the earth
One may be an expert in the eight forms of yoga
One may reach even the moon
But it is impossible to control the body and senses.
Turn the vision inward and achieve the supreme state of
equanimity of mind.

Embodiments of Love!

In this world for a man to accomplish any task, Ichcha Shakthi (will power), Kriya Shakthi (power of action) and Jnaana Shakthi (power of discrimination) are essential. Ichcha Shakthi refers to the determination to undertake a task. Jnaana Shakthi refers to the ways and means to be adopted to fulfil a task. It is not enough if you have Ichcha Shakthi and Jnaana Shakthi;

you need to have Kriya Shakthi too. If you want to weave a cloth, you need to have cotton. The cotton has to be made into threads, which in turn have to be interwoven. This relates to Kriya Shakthi. An enquiry into the type of equipment needed to do this relates to Jnaana Shakthi. Man has all these three potencies in him, but that is not enough. He needs to bring them together.

FUNDAMENTAL AND INCIDENTAL CAUSES

Here is a small example: Supposing you have flowers, thread and a needle; can you have a garland? Should not there be someone to make a garland out of them? You have a container for oil, a wick and a lamp. But, will these alone produce light? No. There must be someone to light the wick. You have gold, gems and precious stones; can you have jewels out of them? No. A goldsmith is needed to make them. Here, you have two types of causes: One is Upaadhaana Kaarana (Fundamental cause) and the other is Nimittha Kaarana (Instrumental cause). A goldsmith makes ornaments using gold, but who is the one who has created gold? He is God. So, God is Upaadhaana Kaarana and Goldsmith is Nimittha Kaarana. Without the primordial principle, Upaadhaana Kaarana (God), Nimittha Kaarana is useless. God, the Upaadhaana Kaarana is the creator of this world. Man, the Nimittha Kaarana is trying to experience and enjoy this creation. But, man forgets the Upaadhaana

Kaarana (God) and thinks he is the doer, and prides himself on his achievements.

Without the primordial basis, man cannot achieve anything. Students of science are aware of this. Two parts of hydrogen and one part of oxygen are combined to make water. Scientists pride themselves on this achievement and ignore God, who is the creator of hydrogen and oxygen. In this modern age, man is carried away by the sense of doership forgetting the Muuladhaara (primordial basis). The potter makes pots, but without clay and water he cannot do so. The potter is only an instrument and hence he is the Nimittha Kaarana and God who has created clay and water is the Upaadhana Kaarana.

BEING - AWARENESS - BLISS

Bharatiyas believe that there are 84 lakhs of species in this world. These can be classified into four categories — 1. Andaja (born out of eggs) 2. Pindaja (born out of womb) 3. Svedhaja (born out of sweat) 4. Uthbhuja (born out of earth). There are 21 lakhs of species under each of these categories. They make a total of 84 lakhs of species. **Beings are many, but the living principle is uniform in all of them.** There are innumerable waves in the infinite ocean, each looking different from the other. Waves may vary in form, but ocean is the basis for all of them.

Likewise, all the 84 lakhs of species have emerged from the ocean of Sath-Chith-Aanandha. All have their origin in Sath-Chith-Aanandha.

What is Sath-Chith-Aanandha? 'Sath' is Being, that which is changeless and eternally present. 'Chith' means Total Awareness. 'Sath' is like sugar, 'Chith' is like water. When water and sugar are mixed, you have neither sugar nor water, but syrup. Similarly, the combination of 'Sath' and 'Chith' results in Aanandha (Bliss). In all the living creatures, you find this Sath-Chith-Aanandha. But man is not able to understand his true identity, which is Sath-Chith-Aanandha and is in search of happiness outside. It is like searching for his own self outside. How can he find his own self outside? He has to look within.

SPIRIT OF ONENESS

In the waking state there are four aspects - Kaala (time), Karma (action), Kaarana (reason), and Karthavya (duty). Suppose you have decided to go to Bangalore by car to participate in a programme. You start at 5 a.m. and reach Bangalore at 8 a.m. Here Kaala (time) is 3 hours, Karma (action) is travelling by car, Kaarana (reason) is the programme and Karthavya (duty) is participating in it. All these four aspects are present in the waking state. Now consider that at 10 o'clock in the night you had a dream.

In the dream you went to Bangalore and participated in a programme. When did you start? How did you travel? When did you reach? What was the reason? You do not know. This only means that the above four aspects do not exist in the dreaming state. In the Sushupthi (deep sleep state), there is no time, no reason, no duty and nothing that you do; you only experience bliss. In the waking state, you undertake different tasks with your body. In the dreaming state, you create everything including your own self. In deep sleep, you enjoy the bliss. You are one and the same in all the three states. On this basis, it can be said that man is changeless in all the three periods of time and experiences bliss directly or indirectly. Man is the embodiment of Trinity. He is essentially Divine. When once he understands this spirit of oneness, there will be no scope for differences and conflicts. So long as you identify yourself with the body, you find only multiplicity.

THREE SINS OF SHANKARA

Once Aadhi Shankara went to Banares and prayed to Lord Vishvanaath thus: "O Lord! I have come here to redeem myself of the three sins I had committed." He had not harmed anyone nor did he steal anything. Then why did he call himself a sinner? He explained the first sin in the following words, "It was I who declared, *Yatho*

Vaacho Nivarthanthe Apraapya Manasaa Saha. Though I know that You are beyond the ken of thought and word, I tried to describe You in a string of words: *Isha, Gireesha, Naresha, Paresha.* I have committed the sin of not practising what I preached. This is my first sin. Though I declared that God is everywhere, I have come all the way to Kaashi to have Your Dharshan (audience) as if You are present only in Kaashi. I have committed the sin of saying one thing and doing another. This is my second sin. It was I who said, *Na Punyam, Na Paapam, Na Sukham, Na Dhukham,* which means there is no merit, no sin, no joy and no sorrow. Yet I am praying for the atonement of my sins. This is the third sin I have committed." The significance of Shankara's statement is the disharmony of thought, word and deed and is in itself a sin. *"Manas Anyath, Vachas Anyath, Karman Anyath Duraathmanaam,"* the evil one is he who does not observe the unity of thought, word and deed. *"Manasyekam, Vachasyekam, Karmanyekam, Mahaathmanaam"*, he is the noble one who has achieved the unity of thought, word and deed.

CHANT THE NAME OF GOD

Every action of Shankara is a teaching to humanity. When he was returning from Banares, he found a person who was trying to memorise Panini's grammatical formula, by constantly repeating, *"Dukrun Karane, Dukrun Karane."*

Shankara decided to give him a teaching. He went and asked him what benefit he would get by repeating Paanini's grammar. That man said that he could become a great Pandith, join the court of the king, and earn lots of money and lead a happy life. When Shankara asked him, what would happen to him after death, he said he did not know. Then Shankara told him, "O foolish man, understand that the body, money and power are temporary. Attain the eternal bliss, which you can enjoy even after your death." Shankara sang the following verse:

"Bhaja Govindam Bhaja Govindam
Govindam Bhaja Moodha Mathe,
Sampraapthe Sannihithe Kaale
Nahi, Nahi Rakshathi Dukrun Karane."

(O foolish man, chant the name of the Lord. When the hour of death arrives, it is only the Lord, who can save you and not your grammar.)

ENGAGE IN SACRED ACTIONS

Though Shankara had no personal gain, he strove hard for the emancipation of humanity. Not only Shankara, Krishna too did the same. In Bhagavath Geetha, He declared:

"Name Paartha! Asthi Karthavyam Trishu
Lokeshu Kinchana
Na anavaaptham avaapthavyam
Vartha evacha Karmaani"

"I don't have to do anything in these three worlds, nor do I gain anything. But yet, in order to teach humanity. I constantly engage Myself in action from dawn to dusk, so that people follow My ideal and sanctify their lives." Only through action man can redeem himself. *"Karmanyeva adhikaarasthe Maaphaleshu Kadhaachana,"* you have got right on action, not on the results. *"Karmaanubandheeni Manushyaloke,"* humanity is bound by action. No one can spend his or her time without invoving in action. When I ask some of the foreigners, what they are doing, they say, they are doing nothing. They think action is related to involving in some kind of job or business. In fact, our inhalation and exhalation process is also a kind of action. Even the movement of eyelids is action. Day in and day out, body is engaged in some kind of action or other. The noblest way is to engage the body in sacred actions such as Shravanam - listening to the Lord's stories, Keerthanam - singing His glories, Smaranam - remembrance, Paadha sevanam - service to the Lotus Feet, Archanam - worship, Vandhanam - salutation, Dhaasyam - servitude, Sakhyam - friendship, Aathmanivedhanam - offering oneself to the Lord i.e., self-surrender.

You should understand that whatever saadhana you do, be it Japa, Thapa, Yoga, Dhyaana or Bhajan - Manthra repetition, Austerities, Sense control, Meditation or Congregational singing - it is for your own satisfaction. God does not need them. Some people think they worship for God's sake; it is a mistaken view. Whatever man does is for his own sake and to meet his selfish ends.

KNOW YOUR TRUE IDENTITY

As you inhale, you make the sound 'So', and when you exhale, you utter the sound 'Ham'. Together 'Soham', means "I am That," which means you are God. When you go on repeating, 'Soham', 'Soham', where is the need for any saadhana? Where is God? How to see Him? These questions of seeing and experiencing God have been there since ancient times. In fact, you have to take to spiritual path in order to know your true reality i.e., Divinity. He is a true aspirant, who knows his true identity. Without realising this truth all spiritual saadhana will be a waste of time.

"Shareeramaadhyam Khalu Dharmasaadhanam," body is gifted to undertake righteous actions. What is our Dharma? Love is our Dharma. Truth is our Dharma. Peace is our Dharma. We should follow our Dharma. The quality of sugar is sweetness; if it is not sweet, it is not sugar. Similarly, Love is your natural quality. Without Love, you cannot be called a human being. There is Love in you. But you are limiting it to your family, friends and relations. But remember that your relations will come with you only upto the burial ground. It is only God, who is with you always, even after your death.

DO KEERTHANA

"*Janthunaam   Narajanma   Durlabham*",
Human life is the rarest. Such a sacred and noble
life should not be wasted. Having taken birth
as a human being, you should set an ideal before
you. A dancer always keeps the rhythm in her
mind, while dancing. Similarly, you should always
remember your innate Divinity in whatever you
do. Maaya (worldly illusion) is like a Narthakee
(dancer) always trying to divert your attention.
In order to control this 'Na-rtha-kee", you have
to do 'Kee-rtha-na' i.e., singing Lord's name.

"*Harernaama, Harernaama Harernaamaiva Kevalam*
Kalau Naasthyeva Naasthyeva Gathiranyathaa"

In this Age of Kali, Lord's name is the only
refuge.

Many people aspire for 'Saakshaathkaara'
(vision of the true Self). Westerners say they
want Liberation. But they do not know what it
really means. If you want to see yourself, you
should give up body attachment and develop
attachment towards the Self. Only then you will
have 'Saakshaathkaara'. At birth, you cry, '*Koham*', '*Koham*', which means 'Who am I? Who
am I?' You should not die with the same question
on your lips. When you die, you should be able
to assert cheerfully, '*Soham*', meaning 'I am God'.
Finding out the answer for the question, 'Who
am I'? is true Liberation.

Today you have endless worries such as birth, death, old age, family life etc. All these are of your own making. They arise because of your attachment and delusion. God does not give them. Who is the giver and who is the receiver, when you are God yourself. So long as you are in 'Bhraanthi' (delusion), you cannot attain Brahman. Just as the ash covers the fire, likewise, Maaya conceals your true identity. Fire is seen when the ash is blown away. Similarly, you can have the vision of the Self, when you give up body attachment.

'I' — FIRST NAME OF GOD

The Vedhaantha says, *"Ekam Sath Viprah Bahudha Vadhanthi"*, Truth is one, but scholars refer to it by many names. The same water has different names in different languages. Similarly, God is One, but He is worshipped in many names and forms. 'I' is the first name of God. Right from the pauper to a millionaire uses the letter 'I' while introducing himself. This 'I' is your true identity. The single letter 'I' refers to Aathma, while the three lettered 'eye' refers to body. Body has three attributes; whereas, the Aathma has none. Aathma is the supreme Bliss. It is the eternal witness and beyond all descriptions. *"Ekaatma Sarvabhootha antharaathma"*, it is the same Divinity that is present in all beings.

CRAVE FOR GOD

Try to enjoy and experience the Love that is in you. If someone says there is no God, tell him, *"May be your God does not exist for you, but my God exists for me. You have no right to question the existence of my God."* You have to argue with such conviction. Such a reply will silence the person. Each one is mad in his own way. The world itself is like a mental hospital. There are some who derive delight in self-praise. There are some that beat and accuse others. But the madness after God is the noblest. God sees to it that you give up the madness for this world and become mad after Him. Only a fortunate few will be blessed with this madness for God. If only the entire humanity develops this madness for God, the world will be rid of disturbances and peace will prevail.

Students! Embodiments of Love!

After every Bhajan session, you are praying for the peace of the world *(Lokaas Samasthaa Sukhino Bhavanthu).* You find only 'pieces', but no peace in this world. In fact, if you develop love and tolerance towards fellow-beings, there will be no need to pray for peace; the world will automaticlly become an abode of peace. Develop love in you and share it with at least ten persons in a day. There are 95 crores of people in this land of Bhaarath. If each one shares his love with others, then all will be one. Out of this unity, you will attain Divinity. Where there is mistake, there is fear; where there is love, there is no fear. **Why fear when I am near and dear.** You should have full faith in Divinity. Many devotees come here, but how many are firm and steady in their faith? All the worldly desires are negative in nature. The negative feelings stand in the way of attaining the positive. So, do not give scope for negative feelings. Develop positive feelings and contemplate on God with unwavering faith.

(Bhagavaan concluded His discourse with the Bhajan *"Hari Bhajana bina sukha shaanthi nahi..."*

(No happiness and peace without chanting Lord's name)

❆ ❆ ❆

LOVE IS GOD; LIVE IN LOVE

(Divine Discourse on 27.9.1998)

Just as dogs bark at mighty elephants,
Some people may heckle the noble souls.
Neither the elephant nor the noble soul
Suffer any loss on this account.

(Thelugu Poem)

Due to the effects of Kali Age, we find many such incidents as mentioned. On hearing the melodious singing of cuckoo birds, crows out of jealousy start cawing at them. But that does not deter the cuckoo from singing. In the same way, seeing the swans, cranes make fun of them. But the swans are least affected. Similarly, the one who has realised his true identity will neither be elated by praise nor depressed by blame.

ADHAMA, MADHYAMA, UTTHAMA

Human life is the gift of God. If only you make proper use of this gift, your life as a human being will find fulfilment. Human beings can be classified into three types: 1. Adhama (low and mean) 2. Madhyama (average) 3. Utthama (noblest). Human body can be compared to a sacred vessel. 'Utthama' is one who makes proper use of this vessel gifted by God. 'Adhama' is one who misuses the body without understanding its value. Madhyama is one who makes use of the body both for sacred and unsacred purposes.

HOW TO EXPERIENCE PEACE AND HAPPINESS ?

What is the use of having a cosy bed, a pillow and a ceiling fan, if one does not get proper sleep ? Likewise, man in spite of being endowed with a heart like a soft bed, a mind like a pillow, and an intellect like a ceiling fan, does not enjoy peace and happiness; then what for are these - the Heart, the mind and the intellect ? We describe the Heart as that which is pure and unsullied. We attribute the quality of all pervasiveness to the mind *(Mano Muulam Idham Jagath)*. We describe the intellect as the transcendental principle *(Atheendhriyam)*. God has gifted these instruments to man, so that he enjoys peace and happiness. In spite of these valuable instruments, man does not have peace and happiness. We say that human life is the rarest and the most precious *(Janthuunaam Nara Janma Dhurlabham)*, but does your conduct deserve such a description ? You are not making proper use of the mind and the intellect, and not keeping the heart pure. As a result, you do not experience peace and happiness. Life devoid of peace and happiness is no life at all.

Great men say that in order to enjoy peace and happiness in life, you need to develop a sense of detachment. Detachment does not mean leading a life of seclusion in a forest, leaving family and property. Students should understand the true spirit of the word 'renunciation'. You should realise that this gross world is inert and consider the subtle aspects of this world as illusion and the causal aspects as only a reflection. Only when you understand the gross, subtle and the causal aspects of the world, you can have renunciation. But man believes this gross world, forgetting the Primal Cause, God.

These three aspects that constitute the apparent world will delude you. You should understand the Primal Cause, the Aathmik Principle. Only then you can experience bliss and peace. You should make an effort to know the value of human life. Human being is called 'Nara'. What is the meaning of 'Nara'? It means embodiment of Atma.

THE FIVE ELEMENTS ARE PRESENT EVERYWHERE

Gopikas used to pray thus: *"Kleem Krishnaaya, Govindhaaya, Gopijanavallabhaaya Svaaha."* 'Kleem' means the earth. 'Krishnaaya' means water. 'Govindhaaya' means fire. 'Gopijanavalla-bhaaya' refers to air. 'Svaaha' refers to ether (Akaasha). There is no life or place in this world without these five elements. They are present everywhere. This is how Gopikas described Krishna as all pervasive. God, who is in the form of five elements is omnipotent, omnipresent and omniscient. So, the main duty of mankind is to make proper use of these five elements. Misuse of these five elements amounts to misuse of Divinity.

TURN YOUR MIND TOWARDS GOD

Man considers his body as everything and spends his entire life in the pursuit of bodily comforts and conveniences. Body is bound to perish. Though 100 year life - span is stipulated, you cannot take it for granted. Death can occur either in boyhood or in youth or in old age. Nobody can say when one would die. Then why should you take such great pains for the sake of your body, which is like a water bubble ? Having taken a human birth, you should lead an ideal life and make everyone happy. You should not give undue importance to the body ; treat it only as an instrument. Mind is like a fan. Only when you turn the fan in your direction, you can enjoy the breeze. Similarly, only when you turn your mind towards God, you can experience the breeze of bliss. But if you turn your mind towards the world and say that you are not able to experience bliss, you are to be blamed. You have to turn your mind towards God, not the body. All the actions that you do for bodily comforts are useless.

You cannot find peace outside, it is within your heart. So, search within. The heart is always filled with peace, love and bliss. It is the basis for all sacred qualities such as compasion, love, tolerance, etc. All that emanates out of your heart is sacred. Body is the root cause for all the six evil qualities (desire, anger, greed, pride, attachment and jealousy). So, do not be attached to the body.

ESCHEW DESIRE, ANGER AND GREED

Human life is very sacred and highly valuable. The mind, the intellect and the senses are mere instruments. But you are not making an effort to know this. You are only trying to understand the nature of the instruments, but not the Aathmik Principle, which is the primordial basis. Your life will be sanctified only when you understand the Aathmik (Divine) Principle. People undertake many spiritual practices in order to sanctify their lives, but without purity of heart all these will be of no use. First, purify your heart. Do not give scope for wicked feelings such as desire, anger and greed. In the spiritual path, these three are worst enemies.

Raavana was one who did great penance and received boons from the Lord. He had mastered all the 64 types of knowledge. Such a mighty and great person like Raavana succumbed to desire and ultimately ruined his life. In the epic Raamaayana, Raavana stands as a symbol of foolishness.

In Bhaagavatha, Hiranyakashipu symbolised anger. He was a great scientist. He had control over the five elements. Modern scientists are able to reach the moon, but Hiranyakashipu could even reach the sun. He even tried to stop the rotation of the earth. Such a great scientist was ruined due to his anger. *The one with anger will never be successful. He ruins his property and loses his respect. He will commit sinful deeds and will be rejected by one and all.* (Poem)

In Mahaabhaaratha, Dhuryodhana stood for greed. *In order to kill a miser, there is no need to harm him physically. Just ask him for money, he will 'die' immediately!* (Poem) Dhuryodhana was such a miser. What could he achieve ultimately? Therefore, for a spiritual aspirant, desire, anger and greed are the worst enemies. The merit acquired through several years of spiritual practice will be ruined in a moment of fury.

OBEY GOD'S COMMAND

In this world, there may be at least one good person out of every ten persons. Out of every ten good persons, there may be at least one who has love for God. Out of every ten persons who have love for God, there may be atleast one who wants to attain Divinity. Out of every ten persons who want to attain Divinity, there may be atleast one who is ever ready to obey God's command. Only he who obeys God's command is redeemed.

There is no point in undertaking spiritual practices without obeying God's command.

GOD, YOUR TRUE FRIEND

Today, everyone wants happiness without understanding what it means. True happiness lies in being desireless. Desire is the cause for misery. A rich man may have no dearth for money, food and other material comforts, but still he may lack peace and happiness. The material objects may provide physical comforts, but not mental peace. Money may give reputation, but not respect. There may be a number of servants, but they are not friends. All serve only out of compulsion, not out of love. There is only one true friend who is always with you, in you and around you. He is God. As long as there is water in the tank, thousands of frogs gather. But once the tank is dry, not a single frog will be seen around. Likewise, so long as you are rich and in position of authority, everyone acts like a friend. But once you lose your position and money, your so-called friends will desert you, without even caring to say good-bye.

In this world, nothing is permanent. Only the principle of love in our heart is permanent. Only love can win people's hearts. If you have love within, the whole world will be with you. What is the reason that so many people from so many countries gather here ? There is something here, which is not there in your country, in your village and in your family. That is the all encompassing love. Only through love, you can establish intimate relationship with each other. The hearts bereft of love are like barren lands. There should be love in the field of human heart. Gopikas prayed to Krishna thus: *O Krishna, play on your flute so that the seeds of Love germinate in the barren fields of our Hearts and make the rains of Love and the rivers of Love flow incessantly.* (Song) Love always gives and never receives. Such selfless Love is only with God. You have gathered here to experience that Love. No one has sent you any invitation. It is only Love that has brought you here.

SPEAK SOFTLY AND SWEETLY

What is it that I am giving you? When I just ask you, "When did you come?", you become ecstatic. There is so much of sweetness even in the words that I utter. You too should learn to speak softly and sweetly. *"You cannot always oblige, but you can always speak obligingly".* Harsh words are like atom bombs. When someone visits your house, even if you do not give anything to eat, at least talk to him sweetly and softly. It can even appease his hunger. Instead, if you speak harshly, that will not only increase his hunger, but also dishearten him.

Charity is the true ornament for the hand.
Truth is the true ornament for the throat.
Listening to sacred texts is the true
                              ornament for the ears.
Why need any other ornaments?
                              (Sanskrith Verse)

You should not have the feeling that only your country should be happy. You should pray for the welfare of the entire world *(Lokaas Samasthaah Sukhino Bhavanthu)*. Let everybody and every country be happy. Only when you have such broad feelings, you will be respected. No one will respect you if your behaviour and words are not proper.

HUMAN LIFE, MOST VALUABLE

Students! Try to understand what human life is? The Upanishaths declared that human life is most valuable. It is not easy to understand the Divine quality immanent in man. All forms and all powers are in man. Man thinks that gold and diamond are most valuable, but actually it is man who endows value to them. *"Men are more valuable than all the wealth of the world".* So, do not waste such a precious human life.

Ancient sages like Vasishttha worked very hard in order to sanctify their life. Why did Vasishttha join the court of Dhasharatha? One day Vasishttha himself explained this to Dhasharatha in the following words: "O king, I have come to you not because you are wealthy and powerful, but because Lord Naaraayana Himself will be born as your son. I want to sanctify my life in His company." Vasishttha always used to contemplate on Divinity. So, he had the appellation, Brahmarishi; whereas, Vishvaamithra was called only a Raajarishi as he was full of Raajasik qualities. In spite of repeated efforts, Vishaamithra could not get the appellation that Vasishttha could get. So, he developed hatred towards Vasishttha. Due to this hatred, Vishvaamithra lost all his powers. You all know that Dhurvaasa, one of the great Rishis, also had the bad quality of anger in him. Even if you were to search with a 'torchlight', you would not find even an iota of love in him. What is the use of being a Maharishi, when there is no trace of love or peace? Only one with sweet words and sacred actions can be called a true Maharishi.

FOSTER HUMAN VALUES

Bharat could progress in ancient times because of saints and noble souls. In spite of repeated foreign invasions, this country could not be destabilised because of the strength of its spiritual power. In order to preserve and sustain the strong spiritual foundation laid by the saints and noble souls, we have to foster human values such as Truth, Righteousness, Peace, Love and Non-violence. If you protect these values, they will in turn protect you. *"Dharmayeva Hatho Hanthi, Dharmo Rakshati Rakshitaha"*. If you protect Dharma, you will be protected by Dharma. Similarly, if you destroy Dharma, you will be killed by Dharma.

DEVELOP LOVE

Love is your true form. Only through love you can achieve anything. There is no need to search for God and no need to undertake any spiritual practice. *"Love is God, Live in Love"*. Without spending a penny and without even crossing your doorstep, you can attain liberation. How? It is only through love. So, develop love. Do not have hatred towards anybody. Start loving even those that abuse you. It is only through love that you can bring transformation in them. By loving them more and more, you can get relieved of the pain inflicted by their harsh words. Harsh words are like sharp arrows that pierce deep into the heart. There is no medicine in this world that can cure you of the pain inflicted by harsh words. When you are shot with the arrows of harsh words, in reply speak sweetly, softly with love. It is the best medicine. It gives quick relief. Any incurable disease can be cured with love.

Embodiments of Love!

What is the cause of disease? It is mental tension, which is man's own making. Tension gives rise to temper and the two together ruin man. If you want to fill a cup with milk, which is already filled with water, what have you to do? You have to pour out the water and then fill it with milk. In the same way, remove all wicked thoughts and wicked feelings from your heart and then fill it with love.

> *"Start the day with Love*
> *Fill the day with Love*
> *Spend the day with Love*
> *End the day with Love*
> *This is the way to God".*

You can develop Love in you by sharing it with others. Love never diminishes. It is nectarine and eternal. Once Naaradha asked Naaraayana if there was anything sweeter than nectar. Naaraayana replied, "Love is sweeter than nectar". You may even get fed up with drinking nectar, but that is not the case with Love. The more you taste it, the more you ask for it. First remove all dirt (bad qualities) in you. As soon as the calf is born, the cow removes all dirt from its body by licking it repeatedly and then feeds it. When a Pashu (animal) has so much of Love for its young one, then you can very well imagine the Love of Pashupathi (God) for His creation. Love cannot be expressed in words. Naaradha said *"Anirvachaneeyam Prema"*, which means Love cannot be described in words.

People think that Naaradha is fond of creating differences *(Kalaha priya)*, but it is a mistaken view. Yes, he was a 'kalaha priya' in his early days, but later on he realised his mistake and did severe penance. He ultimately became a great teacher. It was Naaradha who brought Nara and Naaraayana together. He worked for the attainment of bliss and total removal of grief. He said, "Aathma, the Spirit is God." Love is the principle of God. Having got this Love in you, why should you suffer? Why do you have problems? In fact, you have no difficulties and no anxieties. There is only bliss. But, how can you experience bliss? You have to follow the path of Love. Just by repeating the names of the dishes, your hunger will not be appeased. You have to use your hands and mouth to fill your stomach. In the same way, you have to speak sweet words and do sacred actions. Through these, you will enjoy the sweetness of life and you will be blissful.

DIVINE BLISS IS OUR SOURCE

All are the children of immortality. You are all the embodiments of Aanandha. The Upaniɔnaths say, man is "Aanandha Pipaasi" (seeker of bliss). Since he has emerged from bliss, he wants to return to his source. Just as fish, born out of water, always wants to get into water, so also man, born out of bliss, always craves for bliss wherever he is and whatever he does. Until he returns to his source, man has no rest at all. Man is always restless because he cannot find bliss in this world. That is why The Geetha said, "Anithyam Asukham Lokam, Imam Praapya Bhajasva Maam", this world is temporary, there is no happiness in this world. So chant the name of the Lord. You may engage yourself in your daily activities; there is no need to give up your jobs and business, but keep your mind on God always. Only then you will have peace and happiness. Once you experience Divine bliss, your mind will never crave for worldly pleasures. So, try to experience this bliss, which is within you. **Bliss is your source, bliss is your breath and bliss is your life.**

(Bhagavaan concluded His discourse with the Bhajan, "Govindha Krishna jai, Gopaala Krishna jai..."   (Hail to Krishna!)

�֍ �֍ ✖

GOD IS OUR EVERYTHING

(Divine Discourse on 28.9.1998)

Even a millionarie has to be content with ordinary food,
He cannot live on a diet of gold.
When time is not favourable, a stick may turn into a snake,
While, when it is favourable, dust may turn into gold,
The wheel of time can turn a scholar into a fool and
a fool into a saint.
A wealthy man may become a plaything of adversity at
some time.
Whatever your efforts may be, you cannot get what you
are not destined to get.
O man, don't be over ambitious
Lead instead a noble life making proper use of the intellect.

Embodiments of Love!

In this vast world, among all living creatures, human life is the noblest. One is born as a human being as a result of meritorious deeds done in past lives. Just as a small gramophone plate contains many songs, poems and dialogues; likewise the human heart contains the entire universe in a subtle form. You can neither see the script of the dialogues and songs by keeping the gramophone plate close to your eyes, nor can you hear the sound by keeping it close to your ears. Only by playing it you will be able to hear the music and the dialogues that are in it.

The human heart, which can be compared to a gramophone plate, contains in it all the impressions of past lives. The reaction, resound and reflection of all that you have seen, heard and experienced are contained in it. The infinite oceans, the mighty mountains and all the different places that you visited are imprinted in your heart. In short, the entire universe is imprinted in the human heart. So, it can be said that human being is *Vishva Virat Svaruupa* (Embodiment of Cosmic Principle). But, man not being able to realise this truth considers himself low, and is affected by pleasure and pain, good and bad.

'I' PRINCIPLE

Where from this Universe originated? The Sruthis (Vedhas) have given a proper answer to this. The Universe has originated from where the 'I' principle has originated. That is 'Hridhaya'. Shruthi has declared that 'Hridjhaya' is the origin of 'I' principle. This 'I' is all pervasive. There is no place or person without this 'I' principle.

Even the birds and beasts have got this 'I' principle, though they are not able to express it. Wherever 'I' is, there is 'Hridhaya'. Hridhaya is not limited to body alone, it is all pervasive. 'I' is the name of Aathma. So, in everybody, Aathma is present in the form of 'I'. It is associated with Buddhi (intellect). Right from an illiterate person to a scholar, everyone defines Buddhi as the power to discriminate between the transient and the permanent. This is not the correct definition. Buddhi has five aspects. They are; *Shraddha, Rutham, Sathyam, Yogam and Mahaththathvam.*

MASTER THE MIND AND BE A MASTERMIND

Sraddha has two powers: One is interest and the other is steadfastness. *Rutham* refers to the unity of thought, word and deed. *Rutham* expressed in the form of words becomes *Sathyam.* *Yogam* refers to control over all the senses *(Yogaha Chittha Vritthi Nirodhaha).* The fifth aspect *Mahath - thathvam* is that which is sacred and divine. When Buddhi has all these five aspects, is it not an understatement if we define Buddhi as that which only discriminates between the transient and the permanent?

Today, many talk of Manas (mind) and Buddhi (intellect) without understanding their true meaning. They think that the mind is only a combination of thoughts, but even the actions are associated with it. When the mind and the intellect unite, humaneness reaches a state of freedom, which is referred to as Moksha (Liberation).

It is a mistake to undertake any spiritual practice to control the mind. The nature of the mind is mysterious. It is unsteady and associated with ego. Who can control such a mind? It is impossible. So, never try to control the mind. Follow the intellect, then the mind naturally submits itself. The master of the mind is intellect. The master of the intellect is Atma. Atma has no master. So, *Master the mind and be a Mastermind.*

TRUTH IS ONE

Search for the Truth is search for God, because Truth is God. So, worship Truth, follow Truth and practise Truth. People may deny God, but none can deny Truth. You cannot fragment Truth saying, this is Paakistaani Truth, this is American Truth, this is Indian Truth and so on. Truth is uniform for people of all nations and all religions in all periods of time. Truth is one, so God is one. But you worship God in different forms. This is *Bhraanthi* (delusion). As long as there is *Bhraanthi* in you, you cannot attain *Brahma*. This *Bhraanthi* is the cause for all your sufferings. So, first and foremost give up *Bhraanthi.*

It is a mistake to consider that God is separate from you. Once you become one with God, you can never be separated. For example, a pot full of water emptied in the ocean, becomes one with the ocean. You cannot separate them. Similarly, once you unify your love with God, you become one with God. How to unify? When fire and coal are placed apart, they remain as they are. Only when both are brought close to each other, fire enters coal. If fanning is also done, coal gets transformed into fire. Likewise go closer to God and love Him wholeheartedly. Going close to God can be compared to coal coming in contact with fire (nearness) and loving Him whole-heartedly can be compared to fanning (dearness). Such nearness and dearness to God will ultimately make you one with God. This is what Vedanta declared, *"Brahmavith Brahmaiva Bhavathi"* (the knower of Brahman becomes one with Brahman).

DO NOT MISUSE THE BODY, A TEMPLE OF GOD

Human body contains all the three worlds, Devaloka (head), Naraloka (throat) and Nagaloka (heart). The head is referred to as Devaloka (heaven), as it has got all the five senses of perception that recognise *Shabdha* (sound), *Sparsha* (touch), *Ruupa* (form), *Rasa* (taste) and *Gandha* (smell). *The body is made of five elements and is bound to perish, but the Indweller is immortal. The Indweller has no birth, no death and no bondage. Truly speaking that Indweller is God Himself* (poem). Such a sacred body, the temple of God, is being misused. Yesterday

I told you that the world is made of five elements. Human body is also made of five elements. God is present in the form of five elements all over the world. The Vedas declared: *Anthar Bahischa Thath Sarvam-vyaapya Naaraayana Sthithaha,* which means Divinity is present in you, with you, above you, below you and around you.

BLISS IS WITHIN YOU

A human being has five sheaths: Annamaya Kosha (gross sheath), Praanamaya Kosha (life sheath), Manomaya Kosha (mental sheath), Vijnaanamaya Kosha (wisdom sheath) and Aanandhamaya Kosha (bliss sheath). In order to acquire wisdom, you do not need to go through the sacred texts or hear the teachings of elders. The sacred sheath of wisdom itself is present in you. Once you experience the sheath of wisdom, you will experience the sheath of bliss. Just as the water bubble is born out of water, sustained in it and ultimately merges in water; so also human being is born out of bliss, sustained in bliss and ultimately merges in bliss. But you are not aware of this, wasting your time, money and energy in search of bliss.

Truly speaking, man is wasting a lot of time in wordly pursuits. But he does not spend even a moment to know his Self. "Who am I? What for I am born? What am I doing?" Man does not put these questions to himself. Instead he questions others, "Who are you? Where do you come from? What are you doing?" He has got the inquisitiveness to know about others, but not about himself.

What is the purpose of life? It is not *khaana, peena, sona, marna* (eating, drinking, sleeping, dying). Body is gifted to follow Dharma. Your Dharma is to know your own Self. Consider everyone as divine and the whole world as the mansion of God. Offer all your actions to God. Let every word that you utter be a Manthra and every step you take be Pradakshina (circumambulating God). Instead of leading such a sacred life, man is wasting his time and energy in amassing wealth. What is the value of earning? Truly speaking, nothing. Due to excessive desires, his life has become a big zero.

MAN WITHOUT GOD IS ZERO

Zero gains value when number one (hero) precedes it. As the number of zeroes increases, the value too increases if number one precedes them. Similarly, if you keep God (hero) in view, all the zeroes such as your body, mind and senses also gain value. Hero becomes zero if he forgets God. The world is zero, human life is zero, the sky is zero, the sun is zero and the moon is zero. All these zeroes have got value only because of the Hero i.e., God.

KNOWING ONESELF IS SECRET OF GREATNESS

Take to service, do not think that you are serving others. You are serving only yourself. Similarly, all the spiritual practices such as Japa, Thapa, Dhyaana and Bhajan are for your own satisfaction. God does not need them. God wants only one thing - you should know your Self. Only then you will know God. Confidence in you and confidence in God - this is the secret of greatness. Prahlada had total faith in Narayana, while Hiranya-kashyapu had faith in the body. God will always protect the one with strong faith like Prahlada.

Embodiments of Love!

Today, you visit temples and pilgrimage centres in search of peace, but peace is not found in pilgrimage centres. Peace is not found outside, it is within you. You are the embodiment of Peace, Truth and Love. So search within, tread along the path of Love. Only then you will be peaceful. Through love, you can achieve anything. God is Love, live in Love. Without Love, you cannot be successful. Love helps you to know your Self. In order to experience Love, you do not need to approach anybody, nor do you need to exert yourself. Turn your vision inward.

Krishna said, " *"Mamaiva amsho Jeevaloke Jeevabhuthah Sanaathanaha"* (Human beings are the sparks of the Divine). Serve anybody, it amounts to serving God. The best way to love God is to love all and serve all. If you lead such a life, all your actions will be pleasing unto God.

CULTIVATE SPIRIT OF SACRIFICE

Man needs food clothing, shelter and some money to buy medicines if he were to fall sick. . 's why I said in the beginning, "O man! Never ɔe over ambitious, lead, instead, a noble life by making proper use of the intellect. Happiness lies in contentment. Dissatisfaction will lead to misery. In order to experience peace, keep your desires under control. Misery is the birthplace of all desires. In this journey of life, desires can be compared to luggage. "Less luggage, more comfort, make travel a pleasure." So, reduce your desires. This is called Vairagya (Renunciation). As the desire for the world decreases, the desire for God increases. This is what the Vedhas declared: *"Na Karmanaa, Na Prajayaa, Dhanena, Thyaagenaike, Amruthathvam aanashuh"* (Neither by actions nor by progeny nor by wealth, it is only by sacrifice, one can attain immortality). Offer all your actions to God, consider all as children of God, treat money as God's gift and make proper use of it. So long as you do not develop a spirit of sacrifice, you will have only *Anruthathva* (falsehood). Only sacrifice will give you *Amruthathva* (immortality)

Embodiments of Love!

What is the way to immortality? "Removal

of immorality is the only way to immortality."
Without getting rid of wicked qualities such as
lust, anger, greed and jealousy, how do you expect
to attain immortality? When the tumbler is already
filled with water, you cannot fill it with anything
else. Similarly, when the head is filled with evil
qualities, good qualities have no place in it. You
have filled the vessel of your heart with all types
of worries. Then how do you expect to be happy?
Vyasa gave the essence of all the eighteen puranas
in one sentence, **"Help Ever; Hurt Never."** Only
then you can be happy. If it is not possible to
help, at least do not harm anybody under any
circumstances. You should serve whole-heartedly,
not for name and fame.

CULTIVATE UNITY OF THOUGHT, WORD AND DEED

Today, man is leading a worldly life, giving
up all the ideals. Instead of trying to know his
true identity, he is wasting his time on useless
pursuits. "He knows the route to America, but
not to Kaasi. He knows a lot about Botany, but
not the use of Thulasi plant." What is the use
of leading such a life? Develop Dhaya (Compassion) in your Hridhaya. Today, there is only
fashion, but no compassion. What is the meaning
of mankind? Man should have kindness. The
one without kindness is not a man, but a demon.
"The proper study of mankind is man." There
should be unity in thought, word and deed.
Whatever originates from the heart should be

expressed in words, and the words in turn should be put into action.

DEVELOP DIVINE LOVE TO EXPERIENCE BLISS

Once a devotee prayed thus: "O God, people send many applications to you expressing their desires. Where is the leisure for You to go through all this? When do you reply? We get headache even if we read two letters. But You read many letters and send many replies, yet You remain happy and cheerful. This itself is a sign of Divinity." I am doing all this not for My happiness, but for your happiness. Many people greet Me 'Happy Birthday'. I am always happy. You do not need to greet Me thus. Give happiness to those who are not happy. Happiness cannot be experienced through spiritual practices. It can be experienced only through Divine Love. You will never fail in your life if you have love for God. As the previous speaker said, there are people who have failed for lack of faith, but people with strong faith will never fail. Man is put to suffering because he lacks faith.

In order to experience bliss, you need to develop Love. Love is like a rose and lust is like a thorn. Cut the rose without touching the thorn and offer it to God. You should offer yourself to God. That is surrender. Love within you should be merged with the Divine Love. There lies the bliss.

In Raamaayana, Vaali and Sugreeva suffered because they lacked unity. In the same way Raavana, Kumbhakarna and Vibheeshana also suffered due to lack of unity. Though the Paandavas had difference of opinion among them, they stood united. Therefore, their name and fame spread far and wide. With unity you can achieve anything. There are 95 crore people in India. If there is unity among them, this country can be transformed into very heaven itself. But there is no unity, no purity. Only enmity exists. Heart is like a single chair, not a musical chair or double - seated sofa. So, let Love be seated in that chair, then bad qualities have no place in it. Modern devotion has become artificial. People say something and do quite the opposite. There is no harmony in their thoughts and words. This is not proper. It amounts to cheating themselves.

NO PLEASURE WITHOUT PAIN

Each one has to face one's own destiny. Even Raama had to suffer because of separation from Seetha and the great Paandavas had to live in exile for 12 years. So, you should be ready to face difficulties. There can be no pleasure without pain. Do not feel dejected on seeing a dark night. Think of the moonlight that can be seen on the following night. Similarly, think of the pleasures when you are in pain. Without dark night, there cannot be full moon night. There is happiness in sorrow too. You cannot have happiness out of happiness. You can have happiness only from difficulties.

CONTEMPLATE ON GOD

Though you are the embodiment of Love, you have to necessarily do Sadhana and Seva, till you realise your true identity. Some people say, "Swami, why do we need to be devoted at a young age? We can as well think of God after retirement." When the messengers of death come to seize your life, when your relatives make arrangements to keep your body outside, and when your wife and children cry bitterly, is it possible to remember God at that moment? So, right from an early age, you should contemplate on God. That is why I say, "Start early, drive slowly and reach safely."

Embodiments of Love!

Fight against bad thoughts and bad deeds. Run away from bad company and join good company. Develop good thoughts, good feelings, undertake good actions and attain Divinity.

[Bhagavan concluded His discourse with the Bhajan, *"Hari Bhajana bina sukha shaanthi nahi..."*]

(No happiness and peace without chanting Lord's name)

"MY LIFE IS MY MESSAGE"

(Divine Discourse on 29.9.1998)

Punar Vittham, Punar Mithram, Punah Bhaarya, Punar Mahih,
Ethath Sarvam Punar Labhyam, Na Shareeram Punah Punah

*If man loses money, he can get it back; if he
loses a friend he can get another; if he loses
his wife, even then he can re-marry and have
another wife; if he loses his share of land, he
can get another, but he cannot get back the body
once it is lost.*

ENTIRE HUMANITY IS ONE FAMILY

For all spiritual pursuits, and for and all types
of endeavours in life, body is the main instrument.
Of all the living beings in this world, the human
life is the rarest and most sacred. It is a great
fortune to adorn this vesture of human body.
However in this human body there is mind, which
is mysterious. Everyone is aware of the presence
of the mind in the human body. But, no one
knows the vagaries of mind. Though it does not
have feet to move, it can run faster than air
and light. It has no death, no fixed life span
and always remains youthful. One may be born

again and again, but the same mind follows. Once you understand the nature of the mind, you will be able to understand your true Self.

The whole world is a mansion and the entire humanity is one family. There is no multiplicity. We live under the same sky, tread the same earth, breathe the same air and drink the same water. So, it is foolishness to develop diversity in this underlying principle of unity.

THE WAY TO GOD IS PURITY OF BODY, MIND AND SPEECH

What is the sadhana (spiritual practice) you should undertake? You should purify your body, mind and speech. How to purify the body? It is not enough if it is cleaned with soap and water, which amounts to only external cleanliness. It has to be cleaned with good thoughts, good words, good deeds, which is very essential in the inward path. Whatever work you do, do it with sacred feelings. Divert the body from all unholy activities, use it only for good purposes.

In what way can you purify the mind? You can purify the mind through sense control. Use the ten senses for sacred purposes.

"See no evil, see what is good
Hear no evil, hear what is good
Talk no evil, talk what is good
Think no evil, think what is good
Do no evil, do what is good

This is the way to God".

In order to purify the senses, you should make use of them in a sacred way. Purity of senses is purity of mind. Mind is the master of senses. If the mind is to be pure, senses have to be pure.

How can you purify your speech? You can purify your speech by speaking Truth, following Dharma and culitivating Love and Peace.

'I' IS THE SON, 'MIND' GRANDSON, 'SPEECH' GREAT GRANDSON OF GOD

The moment the human body is born, Aham ('I') also follows it. Aathma is the origin of Aham, so Aham is the son of Aathma. From Aham, mind is born, so mind is the grandson of Aathma. And from mind, speech originates, so speech is the great grandson of Aathma. In short, Aathma, Aham, mind, and speech belong to the same family. So, you should have the conviction that the 'I' principle in you is the dear son of God, mind is the grandson of God and speech is the great grandson. Once you understand that your Aham, mind and speech belong to the Divine family and act accordingly, your life will be sanctified.

Man finds it very difficult to have control over senses. Due to the effect of modern education and high intelligence man has become a slave to his senses. Unable to control his mind, man is leading his life with fear and delusion. From where does this fear arise? Where there is mistake, there is fear. What is the mistake made by man?

He has forgotten that the 'I' principle in him is the son of God. He has forgotten that his mind is the grandson of God and he has forgotten that his speech is the great grandson of God. Since he has forgotten his relationship with God, man is fear-stricken and gripped in anxiety.

Due to the advancement in the field of science and technology, human values are lost and mind has become polluted. On one hand science has progressed, but on the other hand the sanctity of the senses has regressed. Man is happy seeing the advancement in science and technology, but has not realised how far he has moved away from Divinty.

EDUCATION IS FOR LIFE, NOT FOR MERE LIVING

Human life has become artificial. There is no trace of love in his thoughts and in his relationship with others. Even the relationship between mother and son has become artificial. Nowadays when one finds a son talking to his mother, one finds only artificial exchange of words, but not true love. Students are leading an artificial life without sense control. Even the animals have sense control to some extent, but not the modern students. This is due to the progress in modern education. I do not say that education should not progress, I, Myself have established an University. I only say that along with education, students should imbibe good character. Can you call mere bookish knowledge as education ? Can you call all those who read and write educated? Can you call all those who have degrees to their names educated? If education were to be only for a living, do you not find birds and beasts living? Education is for life and not for earning a living. You should study to know the purpose of life. You should not be content with bookish knowledge and superficial knowledge; you should have practical knowledge. To have practical knowledge, enquire within.

BE GRATEFUL TO GOD WHO IS CLOSER THAN MOTHER

You should understand My ideal. Once I say you are Mine, I will never forsake you. You may forget Me, but I will never forget you. You may develop hatred towards Me, but I do not have any hatred towards you. In this world I have no enemies and I have no dislike towards anybody. I always uphold My promise. I always go forward to protect, never do I retreat. But some may question that even after Swami accepts them as His, why do they face problems? Why should they suffer? This is not My mistake. I always keep up My promise. They suffer because they forget their promise and lose their sacredness. I never go back on My word. I never make anyone suffer. Till the last moment, I will be with you, in you, below you, above you and around you. Many are not making an effort to understand this truth. They do not enquire into the reason for their suffering. The change in their heart is the main cause. Their unsteady mind and their ingratitude are responsible for this. The previous speaker Ravi said, God is nearer than your own mother. Though I shower much more love than their own mothers, some people do not show their gratitude. I do not look forward for their gratitude. But when I do My duty, you too have to discharge your duty from your level.

PRAY FOR PEACE OF MIND

Some people blame God for their suffering, ignoring their own defects. They argue saying, God does not keep up His word. God will never go back on His promise. But man does not understand this truth. Being drowned in physical and worldly feelings, he blames God for his suffering. God will never make anyone suffer at any point of time. But each has to face the consequences of his action. Every action has got a reaction. But it may take place immediately, or in a few hours, or in a few days, or in a few months, or in a few years or in a few births. For example, when your finger is cut with a blade, it starts bleeding immediately. When you fall from a staircase, you suffer a fracture. In both the cases, the reactions are instant. The food that you eat takes a minimum of two hours to get digested. For a seed to grow into a tree and yield fruits, it may take a few years. Good or bad, you cannot escape the consequences of your actions. Then you may question, why one should pray to God? One should pray to God not for the alleviation of suffering, but for peace of mind. Once you have peace of mind, all your problems will vanish. You can even escape the consequences of your action if you have God's grace. After the expiry date, the medicine loses its potency; similarly once you acquire God's grace, the consequence of your action will have no effect on you. In order to make the consequence of your action to 'expire', prayer is essential. You have to pray wholeheartedly.

Your Heart is the seat of God. So contemplate on God who is installed in your Heart. You cannot expect happiness in the outside world. Bliss is not in the material world, it is within you. So when you search within, you will find bliss.

Embodiments of Love!

Never blame God for your difficulties. Come what may, pray to Him. That is your duty. So long you have the feeling that you are separate from God, you have to pray. Once you realise that you are one with Him, you need not pray.

INHALE DIVINITY, EXHALE EGO

Your breathing process teaches you a lesson. When you inhale, you make the sound 'So', and when you exhale, you make the sound 'Ham'. This process continues for 21,600 times a day. 'So' refers to Divinity and 'Ham' refers to ego, which means you have to take God into you and drive out Ahamkaram (egotism). This is an important principle of life. We breathe in oxygen and breathe out carbon dioxide. Divinity is like the oxygen, which supports our life and ego is like carbon dioxide, which is dangerous for our health. Ego is a very bad quality. It has to be driven out.

In your daily life, knowingly or unknowingly you are committing mistakes. You are only keeping the physical body clean, but are not making efforts to purify your mind and speech. You are treating bad as good and good as bad. We should make efforts to know what is good and what is bad. All service rendered for the welfare of the society is good. You are a member of the society. So, your welfare depends on the welfare of the society. The country will prosper if the society is good. Individual prayer, family prayer and community prayer, all the three are very essential.

PRAY FOR THE WELFARE OF THE ENTIRE HUMANITY

Vedhas have declared: "Let the whole world be happy". Since ancient times, Bhaarath has propagated spiritual discipline to other countries ensuring peace and security for the entire humanity. You should have such broad feelings. Your love should be as big as an ocean. When Jesus was being crucified, people around were weeping. At that moment an ethereal voice declared: "All are one My dear son! Be alike to everyone." The same thing is taught by the culture of Bhaarath wishing the welfare of the entire humanity. Unfortunately, with the passage of time, selfishness and self-interest have become rampant.

HIMAACHALA MEANS THE PURE HEART

According to Bhaaratheeya culture, Uttharaayana (Northern Solstice) is considered to be very sacred. The great warrior Bheeshma lying on a bed of arrows waited for 56 days for the advent of Uttharaayana to give up his mortal coil. During Uttharaayana, the sun travels towards the north. What does this signify? In the north, we have Himaachala (Himaalaya mountains), which is said to be the dwelling place of Eeshvara. When Eeshvara is all pervasive, how can we limit him to Himaachala. What is the significance of this statement? The word 'Himaachala' is made up of two words: *'Hima'+ 'Achala'. 'Hima'* means that which is white as snow. *'Achala'* is that which is firm and unshakable. What is the place to which this description applies? It is the pure Heart, where Eeshvara is installed. It is said, *"Eeshvara Sarva Bhuuthanaam"*, which means Eeshvara is the indweller of all beings. So, in order to see God, you do not need to go anywhere, turn your vision inward. We cannot call an unsteady and impure heart as Himaachala. Only the Heart, which is pure, sacred, unpolluted, and unwavering can be called Himaachala.

PARENTS, TEACHERS - SET A GOOD EXAMPLE

There is no trace of spiritual thinking among modern students. When the parents and teachers themselves have not realised the importance of spirituality, how can we blame the students. First the parents must teach their wards to pray to God everyday. But the modern parents themselves do not pray to God. As soon as they come from office, they go to clubs and spend their time playing cards and drinking. Naturally, children follow their footsteps. In some houses, parents quarrel in front of their children, which is an unhealthy practice. If there is any difference of opinion among parents, they should resolve it in the absence of their children. Children cannot concentrate on their studies if they are disturbed by the family problems. So, parents should never discuss them in front of their children. There are a few parents who set a bad example to their children by speaking untruth. For example, if some unwanted person makes a phone call, they instruct their children to tell him that they are not available. Thus, they encourage their children to utter lies.

Some children are like pure gold as long as they are here. Once they go for a vacation, their minds get polluted. But, some students remain the same. Some return much before their vacation ends in order to spend time with Bhagavaan. It is the innate culture acquired as a result of deeds done in past lives that shapes their behaviour.

Students! Embodiments of Love!

You should try to know what Divinity is. In this age of science, some say that there is no God. But there is God in all periods of time. There is no oᴜᴇr matter. *"Yath Dhrishyam Thannashyam"* (Whatever is seen by the naked eye is bound to disappear). Only God is permanent.

"MY LIFE IS MY MESSAGE"

Time is most precious in human life. Misuse of time is evil. "Time is God, so don't waste time. I feel very sad when I find you wasting time. *I always say, "My life is My message." I never waste even a moment. You think that after dining Swami goes and sleeps. But, actually I do not know what sleep is. I never sleep. As you know, I collect letters from you. I see some of them immediately. I spend time in a most sacred way. But I do not require anything. I do not need anything in all the three worlds. I do not need anything for Myself. Still, I am engaged in activity from dawn to dusk in order to set an ideal. From top to toe, there is no trace of selfishness in Me. Believe it or not, I always spend My time for others. I always give, but never receive. I ask for only one thing and that is Pure Love. I am ready to give My life for those who offer their pure love. You cannot understand My work. Only men of sacrifice can understand this. I am always engaged in activity. I do something or the other. Even While resting I am working. I have to take rest for others' sake. Otherwise they too do not take rest. To give them rest, I take rest. What is My rest? Doing devotees' work is My rest.*

SVAAMI TAKES UPON HIMSELF A DEVOTEE'S HEART ATTACK

The previous speaker Narsimhamurthy spoke about this incident. One day all of a sudden I left this body. Gangadhar Shetty, Narsimhamurthy were surprised at this. Only these two were there inside as it was not possible for others to come in. I told them: "There is a widow who always thinks of Svaami. She has two children. After the death of her husband, she took up a small job to maintain her family. She sustained a heart attack. The loss of her husband and her inability to run the family made her depressed. As the money was not sufficient she joined a part-time job. But every moment she used to chant the name, Sairaam, Sairaam, Sairaam... whole-heartedly. In such a situation, she suffered a heart attack. In fact, she was to die. So I took over her heart attack on Myself. For seven long days I did not come down. I took upon Myself all her sufferings and pain and made her healthy. After three days she sent a telegram, "Svaami,

You came and protected me and my children."
She did not know that I had taken her disease
on Myself. After a week, she came with her
children.

SPIRITUALITY IS PRESENT ALL OVER THE WORLD

I am ready to do anything for the sake of
those who have total Faith and pure Love. But
it is very difficult to find such devotees. However
there are a few of them. If there are no noble
people, how is it that you find daylight in this
world? There are many sacred people in this
country as well as in this world. Do not limit
spirituality to Bhaarath, it is present all over the
world. Truly speaking it is more in foreign
countries, than in Bhaarath. Indians do not know
what is Brahmasuuthras, Upanishaths and Bhagavath Geetha. But, the foreigners have learnt
Bhagavath Geetha by heart.

JOIN GOOD COMPANY

In Italy, there is a devotee who has learnt
Brahmasuuthras by heart. She can chant Rudhram.
There, she has constructed a building by name
'Mother Sai', spread over 25 acres of land. Having
full faith that one day Svaami will certainly visit
that place, she has also built a spacious hall
like Puurnachandra Auditorium, so that public
meetings could be held there. She also has
constructed some rooms to accommodate students that follow Svaami. Do you know, how

clearly our Primary School children from foreign countries chant the Vedhas! This is the result of being in good company. If the company is good, children's future also will be good. *"Tell me your company, I shall tell you what you are."* As is your company, so you become. So, wherever you go, join good company. Let your heart and mind be purified. Speak always truth in a palatable and acceptable way. This is the spiritual path which you have to adopt.

People may wonder as to why one should do meditation and bhajans. They are all good actions meant to sanctify the time, but God is not interested in them. What is that you should do to make God happy? You should involve your body in good deeds. Fill the mind with good thoughts and speak sweetly and softly. Only these actions please God. Bhaaratheeyas refer to this as *'Thrikaranashuddhi''* (Unity of thought, word and deed). With sacred feelings, students should undertake sacred actions and lead an ideal life. This is what I teach the students in particular.

EXPRESS YOUR GRATITUDE TO THE INSTITUTE

Those students who study here should transform thousands of students outside. It is not enough if you merely preach, first practise what you preach. Only then your study in this Institute will find fulfilment. We do not receive even a naya paisa from you. Education is offered free. How can you express your gratitude to this Institute? Share with others all that you have learnt here. This is the true gratitude. Do your jobs, take care of your parents. Fill your Hearts with Divinity. When there is pure water in tank, you get the same water out of the taps. Your Heart is like a tank. All the senses are like taps. So, fill your Hearts with love,and experience love. I expect and bless the students to take to this path of Love and lead an ideal life. Thus, I bring My discourse to a close.

Bhagavan concluded His Divine discourse with the Bhajans: *"Bhavabhaya harana vandhitha charana" and "Subrahmanyam, Subrahmanyam ..."*
(Oh God! Remover of worldly illusion, and whose feet are worthy of adoration)

POWER OF DIVINE LOVE

Divine Discourse on 30.9.1998

Nirguno Nishkriyo Nithyo Nirvikalpo Niranjanaha
Nirvikaaro Niraakaaro Nithya Mukthohi Nirmalah

*Attributeless, unattached to work, ever pure in
mind, ever blissful, unsullied and formless. He
(the absolute) is eternally liberated and pure.*

There is one principle, which is attributeless,
formless, eternal and beyond thought, word and
action. That is the principle of Love. Upanishaths
call this Love, Aathma. How can man understand
this Love, which is attribute-less and formless?
This Love is not an intellectual exercise, nor is
it psychological; nor is it a reflection in the
dreaming state. It is the life principle of all living
creatures. Noble souls propagated this principle
of Love in various ways. Many elders, youngsters,
scholars lecture on this principle of Love and
sing its glory. But, no poetry, no composition,
no language can describes Love. *Yatho Vaacho
Nivarthanthe Apraapya Manasaasaha",* Love cannot be described in thought and word. It is
beyond human comprehension and narration.
Love has no form, it can be seen only in practice.

If one is to ask, what is the form of Love, it can be said Love is God. Who is God? Where is God? What is His form? How to search Him? This has been the constant enquiry since ancient times. But, none can describe Divinity. Vedhas said: *"Vedhaaham Etham Purusham Mahaantham Aadithyavarnam Thamasah Parasthaath"* (Divinity shines with the brilliance of thousand Suns, beyond the darkness of ignorance). Divinity is beyond human understanding and expression.

LOVE ALL AND MAKE ALL HAPPY

How can one recognise Divinity who is the embodiment of Love? In this world Love assumes various forms, as expressed by mother, father, brother, wife, friends and relations. In this wordly love you find selfishness and self-interest. But the Divine Love is absolutely selfless. Just as God loves all, you should also make efforts to love all, because in the Bhagavath Geetha, God says, *"Mamaivaamsho Jeevaloke Jeevabhoothah Sanathanaha",* which means all are the sparks of the Divine. So, as He loves you, you should also love all and make all happy. But, today one does not find such love between human beings. Divine Love does not expect anything in return. In order to cultivate such Divine Love, man should have the faith that he is the spark of the Divine and He should understand that the same God is present in all. Once he understands and develops faith in this truth, he can love everybody. Today one does not find such love, it only means that man has no faith in the statement of God *(Mamaivaamsho...)*

DIVINITY PERVADES EVERY WHERE

Just as a Mariner's compass always points towards north, likewise under all circumstances Love is directed towards God. Time, space and individuals do not affect Love. Love is the true sign of Divinity. Understanding Love amounts to understanding Divinity. None can decide the form of God. When you enter a cinema theatre, you find a white screen. Merely watching the screen does not satisfy you. Once the show commences, you find different characters projected on the screen. Without the screen, can you see the picture? No. But, when the picture is projected, though the screen exists, it is not seen. The screen exists all the time - before, during and after the show. Vedas declared: *"Anthar Bahischa Thath Sarvam Vyaapya Naraayana Sthithaha"* (God is present within and around). Like the screen is to the picture, so is the Atma for the creation. The screen of Atma is present within and around all beings and it is the primordial basis for the entire creation. Therefore, it is said: *"Sarvam Vishnumayam Jagath"* (Divinity pervades everywhere). Divinity is present in the 'picture', around the 'picture'. So, who can decide the form of such Divinity?

On the screen of Love, you find the picture of the universe. This Love is present in the name of Atma in all the beings. What form can you attribute to the Love present in you? It is not possible. How can a person who does not understand his true nature, understand God? So first and foremost one should make efforts to understand one's own Self.

SAME AATHMA IS IN ALL BEINGS

The Aathma has no definite name and form. *"Ek Prabhu ke anek naam"* (The one Lord has many names). Aathma is the fundamental principle, which is pure, steady and unsullied. It forms the basis for the entire universe. Without the basis of the Aathma, the universe cannot exist. Vedhas declared: *"Pashyannapi Napashyathi Muudho"* (he is a fool who sees yet does not see). The same principle of Aathma is reflected in all beings. God is the basis for the entire universe. It appears rather mysterious when we enquire where God is? God is in forest and also in mansion. He is present in your Heart and also in your speech. He is present everywhere. So, never make an attempt to comprehend Divinity. Instead have faith in God, follow Him, worship Him and experience bliss.

In order to experience Divinity, understand this example. The very nature of mother is love. Mother has a form, but Love has no form. Mother herself is the form of love. Due to the presence of the Aathmik principle, you are able to see its reflection in the form of world. The whole world is nothing but reflection, reaction and resound. Aathma is the reality. But man has forgotten the reality and is seeing only the reflection. You cannot have reaction without action, you cannot have resound without sound. Though the Sound is everywhere, you are not able to hear it. Though the Reality is everywhere, you are not able to see it. How to see it? With unflinching faith and selfless love, contemplate on God constantly. God will certainly manifest before you.

DEVELOP SELF - CONFIDENCE

Today man chants the name of God and desires to see Him. But as he lacks steady faith, he is not able to experience Divinity. Man has become blind having lost the two eyes of faith. Faith is most important. Self-confidence is the foundation on which one can build the walls of self-satisfaction. On the walls of self-satisfaction, one can lay the roof of self-sacrifice. Under the roof of self-sacrifice, one can lead a life of self-realisation. You cannot have walls without foundation and roof without walls. So self-confidence, the foundation, is very important.

Today man pretends as if he has love, but does not know what it is. Our Vice-chancellor described Svaami's Love as that of thousand mother's love. But the one who cannot understand the love of one mother, how can he understand the love of thousand mothers. So, first and foremost try to understand and experience the love of your physical mother. This is the significance of Mother worship in this Navaratri.

GOD'S MULTIFARIOUS CREATION

The culture of Heart is the standard of life. What is this culture? It is the divine feeling that originates in the Heart. All the materials and powers of the world are present in your Heart. Men may vary in name and form, but the cultural principle of the Heart is one and the same. God resides in this Heart. What is His form? The Vedhas describe Him as formless, attributeless, ancient and eternal. No one can attribute a name to God. Had anyone existed before God, they would have named Him. But, none existed before God. Creation itself did not exist.

For crores of years, there existed only darkness. At that time, the sun and the moon did not exist and there was no living creature. Nothing was seen. Then it rained heavily for lakhs and lakhs of years. This resulted in the formation of oceans. From the oceans, rivers originated. Then there was light in this world, and one could see the sun and the moon. Human habitation came into existence only after this entire process, which took place for many crores of years. Then how do you expect man to understand Divinity?

First and foremost man has to kill the Thaamasik quality in him. Though water has no colour, it appears red when poured into a red bottle. Similarly, the Aathmik principle, which is pure and unsullied, appears 'red' in a person with Raajasik quality; 'dark' in a person with Thaamasik quality and 'bright' in the Heart of a person with Saathvik quality.

In the Bhagavath Geetha, Krishna said He created four 'Varnas' *(Chaathurvarnyam Mayaa Shrustam)*. But people mistake these four varnas for four castes - Braahmana, Vaishya, Kshathriya and Shuudhra. Here Varna refers to the colour, but not to the caste. Russians are red-complexioned, British are white-complexioned, Japanese are yellow-complexioned and the Africans are dark-complexioned. The remaining colours are only the combinations of these four colours.

SIGNIFICANCE OF CHANTING FOOD PRAYER

Students chant a prayer and offer the food to God before they partake of it. How do they pray?

"Brahmaarpanam Brahmahavir
Brahmaagnou Brahmanaahutham
Brahmaivathena Ganthavyam
Brahmakarma Samaadhinaa"

They think they are offering the food to Brahma. But, where is Brahma? He is right within.

He gives immediate response. What is it?

"Aham Vaishvaanarobhoothva
Praaninaam Dehamaashrithah
Praanaapaana Samayukthah
Pachaamyannam chathurvidham"

What does this mean? It means, Brahma who is present in the form of Vaishvaanara in you digests the food that you partake. Who is responsible for your blood circulation? Who makes your heart beat for 24 hours a day? It is all God's creation. None can understand this. In His creation God has a special place for human beings. He has endowed them with Constant Integrated Awareness *(Prajnaanam)*. Vedhas declared: *"Prajnaanam Brahma".* (Brahman is Constant Integrated Awareness).

BUDDHI GREATER THAN MEDHA SHAKTI

Once, King Vikramaadithya convened a meeting of scholars. He asked them, which is greater among the two — Buddhi (intellect) or Medhaa Shakthi (brain power)? The scholars came to a conclusion that Buddhi is greater than Medhaa Shakthi. They said Medhaa Shakthi is only worldly intelligence, which is temporary; whereas, Buddhi consisted of five aspects — Shraddha, Sathyam, Rutham, Yogam and Mahath Thathvam. All the worldly achievements are based on Medha Shakthi, but not on Buddhi. Buddhi is transcendental and beyond all the senses. It relates to Nivritthi Maarga (inward path); whereas, Medhaa Shakthi relates to Pravritthi Maarga (outward path).

FILL YOUR HEART WITH LOVE

The principle of Love is the most important of all. Love is Atma, Love is Wisdom, Love is Truth, Love is Righteousness, Love is Peace and Love is Non-violence. Where there is Love, untruth, violence and restlessness find no place. Human heart is a single chair, but not a double sofa, or a musical chair. So, once you fill your Heart with Love, wicked feelings have no place in it. Everything is contained in Love. Love is the life principle. But man has forgotten this principle of Love and is wasting his time in worldly love. The love between the mother and child is Vaatsalya (maternal love); the love between wife and husband is Moha (attachment). It is only the Divine Love that is the true Love in the strict sense of the term. Love applies to God only, none else.

Praachethasa (Vaalmeeki) composed Raamaayana consisting of hundred crores of verses. Dhevathas (demi-gods), Raakshasas (demons) and Maanavaas (human beings) came to know that whoever goes through Raamaayana and follows its teachings, would be liberated. Immediately they approached Brahma and requested Him for a share of Raamaayana. Brahma divided

Raamaayana into three parts consisting of 33,33,33,333 verses each and distributed to them. One verse consisting of 32 letters remained. Then Brahma again divided these letters into three parts consisting of ten letters each and distributed to them. Ultimately two letters remained. These are the two letters of the holy names of God — Raama, Krishna, Hari, Shiva, Sai and Baba, which were equally given to them. For all these names the primordial principle is Love.

UNDERTAKE SACRED ACTIONS

Only through Love world peace can be achieved, non-violence can be practised. Buddha said, non-violence is the supreme dharma. He did penance for six years. He approached elders and listened to their teachings, but he could not get any benefit out of them. Ultimately he enquired within and found out the Truth. He said Samyak Drishti (sacred vision) led to Samyak Bhaavam (sacred feelings) which in turn led to Samyak vaak (sacred speech). Samyak Vaak (sacred speech) led to Samyak Karma (sacred action). Spiritual Sadhana does not mean doing meditation or Japa. Undertaking sacred actions is the true sadhana. Krishna said: *"Karmanyevaadhikaarasthe Maaphaleshu Kadhaachana"*, you have got right on action but not on the results. Human society is bound by action. So undertake good actions.

MAKE PROPER USE OF BODY, MIND, INTELLECT

Today, man does not make an effort to know why the body is gifted. The body is gifted not

for just 'loading' and 'unloading'. Food is required
to keep the body fit to undertake sacred actions.
As is the food, so is the head. As is the head,
so is God. So partake of sacred food, undertake
sacred actions and join good company. To the
extent possible, render service to the society. Have
good feelings in your Heart, speak good words
and do good actions. This is called Trikaranashu-
ddhi (unity of Heart, word and deed). Understand
that this is the purpose of human life. Whatever
actions you undertake, do them to please God
(Sarvakarma Bhagavath Preethyartham). Divinity
pervades everything, right from an ant to Brahma,
but man does not realise this and misuses his
body. Body is the gift of God. To misuse it
is a great sin. Sin and merit are not present
in a foreign land; they are attached to your actions.
Good actions yield good results and bad actions
yield bad results. Therefore make proper use
of the body, mind and the intellect, which are
the gifts of God.

SERVICE UNTO OTHERS IS SERVICE TO GOD

What is Saadhana ? Service is true Saadhana.
Serve the society. Treat everyone as your brothers
and sisters. Only through selfless service, your
life will be redeemed. Consider service unto others
as service to God. Unfortunately today man takes
to service expecting something in return. He has
become money-minded. Excessive wealth makes
one egoistic. Ego leads to bad qualities. Excessive

desires make one suffer. As the desire increases, misery too increases. *"Asamthruptho Dhvijo Nashtah"*, a discontented man suffers both ways (i.e. he is not happy with what he has and feels unhappy over what he has not). So, be contented with what you have. Experience bliss and share it with others. If you have devotion, God Himself will confer bliss.

FOLLOW THE COMMAND OF GOD WITHOUT DOUBTS

As our Vice-chancellor said, when Raama asked Hanumaan to go to Lanka, Sugreeva, Jaambavantha and others doubted if he could cross the ocean. Then Hanumaan smilingly replied that as Raama Himself commanded him to cross the ocean, He would also grant the necessary strength. He leaped across the ocean chanting the name of Raama and reached Lanka. Having been commanded by Raama, he never doubted whether he could accomplish the task. Once God commands you to do something, He will certainly grant the necessary skill and strength. So act according to the command of God without a trace of doubt, you will certainly be successful.

Today as science is progressing, doubts are also increasing in the human mind. The more intelligent you are, the more doubts you have. So do not aspire for more intelligence (Medhaa Shakthi). Make proper use of the intelligence given by God.

SAI GRANTS DEVOTION, STRENGTH AND LIBERATION

Happiness lies in union with God. God is the embodiment of Bliss, which is eternal, unsullied, pure and non - dual. It is most unfortunate if you forget God. *"Never give up Sai and make the best use of the chance given. Once you lose the opportunity to serve the Lotus Feet of Partheesha, you will not get it back. Sai grants you devotion, strength and liberation. Do not ruin yourself by listening to others."* Do not believe anybody; believe your conscience and follow it. Once you follow your conscience, you will attain consciousness, Aathma. Develop self - confidence, worship God, attain Divinity and be an ideal to the rest of the world. That is the essence of education.

"The man who studies and studies without discrimination fails to understand Himself. A mean-minded man can never give up his meanness, in spite of his vast learning. Why should one waste one's life in the pursuit of acquiring bookish knowledge? Better it is to acquire such wisdom that confers immortality."

The worldly education leads to argumentation, but not total knowledge. It is all a waste of time. It is a sign of ignorance. So never argue with anybody. *"Vaadhe, vaadhe Varthathe Vairam"*, arguments will lead only to enmity. Today what we need is unity, purity and divinity.

YAGNA IS FOR WORLD'S WELFARE

For the last seven days you are a witness to this holy yagna. Why is it conducted? It is for the welfare of the world. The name of God should spread everywhere. For example, Delhi is far away from here, but when you tune your radio to a particular wavelength, you can hear the songs that are being broadcast in Delhi station. This is possible because of the presence of electric waves in the atmosphere. All over the world there are electric waves and magnetic waves. So the effects of manthras chanted during the yagna will spread all over the world and purify the atmosphere. Once the manthras enter the air that you breathe in, you will develop sacred feelings, because there is also a manthra in you. The body is yanthra, Hridaya is thanthra and the breath is manthra (Soham). Soham means, "I am God". There is no greater manthra than this. Therefore, chant this sacred manthra, lead an ideal life and make the world an abode of peace.

Embodiments of Love!

In this train of society, youths are the long journey passengers. As the youths have a long way to go, they should work for world peace. Teach the principle of Divinity. Instil Divine feelings even in hard-hearted people. Sow the seed of the holy name of God in every heart. Then the world will become verily the heaven. Your happiness is heaven; your grief is hell. So be happy and serve everybody. Do not have the narrow feeling that only Bhaarath should be prosperous; pray for the prosperity of the entire world because all are your brothers and sisters. Have such broad feelings and sacred thoughts. Only then the dictum *"Lokaas Samasthaah Sukhino Bhavanthu"* will be realised, everyone will be happy. Share this immortal principle with every body.

LEAD A LIFE OF SACRIFICE

Upanishaths address you as the sons of immortality *(Shrunvanthu Vishve Amruthasya Puthraah* - listen O children of immortality*)*. You should lead your life befitting your name. Thyaaga-raaja said, *"Nidhi Chaala Sukhamaa, Eeshvara Sannidhi Chaala Sukhamaa, Nijamuga Thelupumu Manasaa"*, O mind tell me, is it money or proximity to the Divine that confers happiness. He rejected the money sent by the king saying Raama is his only wealth. Thyaagaraaja means one with sacrifice. So his action befitted his name. There is no heaven beyond sacrifice. Do not have excessive desire for wealth. Lead a life of sacrifice. Lead a peaceful life.

(Bhagavan concluded His discourse with the Bhajan: *"Prema mudhita manase kaho Raama Raama Raam..."*)
(Chant the name - RAAMA - with a love filled heart)

DEVELOP STEADFAST FAITH IN GOD

(Divine Discourse on 1.10.1998)

Dhaivadheenam Jagathsarvam Sathyaadheenamthu Dhaivatham
Thath Sathyam Utthammaadheenam Utthamo Paradhevatha

The whole world is governed by God
and God is governed by Truth;
Truth is in the hands of noble souls,
and the noble souls are verily Divine.

Embodiments of Love!

Since ancient times our country of Bhaarath
has been spreading the infinite spiritual knowledge
to every country all over the world. Bhaarath
believes that for the peace and security of the
entire world, spirituality is most essential. Bhaara-
thiyas, with all the sincerity and devotion have
made efforts to establish stability and peace in
the world. But, with the passage of time, due
to the effects of Kali Age, people have lost faith
in the Self, and have reposed faith in this transient
and ephemeral world. Today man does not have
even the Self - confidence of birds and beasts.
When a small bird rests on a thin branch of
a tree, the branch starts tossing up and down.

But the bird is not fear-stricken because it depends on its wings, not on the branch it rests. Bird has total reliance on its wings, but not man in his Self; he suffers as a result.

DEVELOP FAITH IN THE SELF

In spite of the fact that man goes through sacred texts and listens to the discourses, he has not developed faith in the Self. He nods his head as he listens to the discourses with the feeling of having understood and benefited by them, but does not have the faith to put them into practice.

There is no scope for any doubt in a man with faith in the Self. He is unperturbed by the vicissitudes of life. Since ancient times, the culture of Bharath has had Self-confidence as the basis. But with the commencement of the modern age, the Self-confidence is on the decline. Every man should develop faith in the Self. One can attain the blissful state only through Self-confidence.

Today is Vijaya Dhashami. This is the Samaapthi (conclusion) of sacred Navaratri festival. Samaapthi is that which confers Praapthi (deservedness) in every possible way. This also happens to be the day on which Shirdi Baba left his mortal coil. Having left His mortal coil on this day, Shirdi Baba re-incarnated here after 8 years. This is an ample testimony to the existence of Divinity in humanity.

If man does not know his own Self, what is the use of knowing the rest? He reads newspaper everyday in order to be aware of the happenings around the world. He makes efforts to know what is happening in every country, but does not put in any effort to know his own Self. He keeps questioning whosoever he comes across, "Who are you? Where do you come from?", but he does not put these questions to himself. There is no point in undertaking any spiritual practice without Self-enquiry.

Food and habits play a vital role in fostering the human values. As is the food, so is the head. As is the head, so is God. You should understand the connection among food, head and God.

DHRAUPADHI'S LAUGHTER

Today we find many unhealthy changes in the food and habits of man. This is the main cause for the lack of purity of Heart. After the Paandavas emerged victorious in the battle against Kauravas, Krishna took them to Bheeshmaachaarya, who was lying on a bed of arrows, for his counsel and blessings. Bheeshma began expounding to them all aspects of Dharma. This teaching of Bheeshma is called Shaanthi Parva in Mahabharatha. When all Paandavas were listening to their grandsire with all sincerity and devotion, Dhraupadhi suddenly burst into laughter. But one should be aware of the fact that Dhraupadhi was one of noble virtues and sense of discrimination. She was one who practised the cultural values of Bhaarath. But all the Paandava brothers were very much upset by her unaccountable levity and considered it as an insult to the venerable Bheeshma. Bheema and Arjuna became very furious and Dharmaja bent his head in shame. But Bheeshma knew the reason for Dhraupadhi's laughter. He called her close and said, "My dear child, the people of this world are like crows and will misinterpret your laughter in varied ways. Without trying to know the truth, they will misunderstand and misinterpret. So explain the reason for such a behaviour and thereby remove the misapprehension of your husbands".

She replied "Revered grandsire! You should have taught these lessons of Dharma to the evil-minded Kauravas. But instead, you are teaching now to my husbands, who are virtuous, righteous and selfless. This appeared to me both ironical and futile. Hence I could not refrain from laughing."

BAD COMPANY AFFECTED BHEESHMA'S MIND

Then Bheeshma said, "Dhraupadhi, I can understand your feelings, but as I have been living in the company of Kauravas, my blood and mind have become polluted as a result of consuming food from such wicked persons. Knowing fully well that Kauravas were on the wrong side, I have not corrected them. But, as good luck would have it, Arjuna's arrows have drained away all that impure blood from me in the last 56 days. As a result the good thoughts and good feelings that were lying buried deep in me are coming out." It was bad company that affected Bheeshma's mind. This fact is very well expressed by the statement, "Tell me your company, I shall tell you what you are." As is the company, so you think and so you become.

Every teaching has to be passed on keeping in view the time, space and circumstances. Though Krishna and Arjuna moved together for 64 years before Kurukshethra war, never did Krishna mention anything about Bhagavath Geetha to Arjuna. It was only before the war that Krishna gave the teaching to Arjuna. For everything there is an appropriate time.

DISPEL BAD THOUGHTS

You might have gone through many sacred texts and heard many sacred teachings. You may also have had the darshan of sacred people. What is the use? Due to the effect of unsacred food and bad company, all your good thoughts are subdued. Good thoughts can express themselves only when you get rid of bad thoughts. Everyone must make an effort to dispel bad thoughts.

Consider this example, you have built a house with a main door and many windows for proper ventilation. Just because there is an entrance you will not allow all the street dogs and pigs into your house. You open the door only for your family, friends and relatives. Likewise mind is the main door and senses are like windows to the body, which is the temple of God *("Deho Devaalayah Proktho Jeevo Dhevah Sanathanah"*- The Body has been described as a temple and the indweller as the eternal Divine. You have to enquire as to who is to be permitted into this temple and who is not to be permitted. But today no one makes this enquiry. As a result all types of wicked feelings and wicked thoughts are permitted to enter the mind.

HAVE LIMITED CONTACTS

'Nasreyo Niyamam Vinaa", for everything discipline is essential. You should not develop friendship with whosoever you come across. You should enquire whether the person is good or not. However, do not hate anybody (Adhveshta Sarvabhoothaanaam). At the same time do not cross your limits in your dealings with others. Have limited connections and contacts.

What is the use of being born as a human being, if you do not foster human values such as Sathya, Dharma, Shaanthi, Prema and Ahimsa ? The Vedas say "Sathyam Vadha; Dharmam Chara," Speak truth and follow righteousness. Peace is like a precious jewel to mankind. Saint

Thyaagaraaja said, "Shaanthamu leka soukhyamu ledu", without peace there is no happiness in this world. For all the human values, Love is the basis.

Today, human beings are human in form but not human in practice. In some places one finds people exhibiting human values outwardly, without practising them whole-heartedly. Human values are not meant for Pradharshana (exhibition), but are meant for Nidharshana (example). Human values should be reflected in all your thoughts, words and deeds. But today, there is only selfishness and self-interest in whatever man thinks, speaks and does. Due to selfishness and self-interest, human values are totally lost.

A small example, here you find many bulbs glowing. It is not enough you have bulbs, you also need to have wires and current. When the current flows through the wires and enters the bulbs, they start glowing. Likewise, in order to experience the light of Love, the current of Truth has to pass through the wires of Dharma and enter the bulb of Peace.

UNIFY THOUGHT, WORD AND DEED

As I have already told you, Aathma is the origin of Aham, Aham is the origin of mind and mind is the origin of speech. So, Aham is the son of Aathma, mind is the grandson of Aathma and speech is the great grandson of Aathma.

First and foremost you should remember that Aathma, Aham, mind and speech belong to the same family. So, Aham, mind and speech should be filled with the feelings of Aathma. Only when there is a total unification of Aham, mind and speech with Aathma, you will become a total human being. When Aathma is the underlying principle in Aham, mind and speech, there is no scope for any mistake. But today there is no Aathmik feeling in man's thought, word and deed. This is the cause of all suffering

UNITY IN DIVERSITY

You should develop the spirit of nationalism and practise ancient Bhaarathiya culture. The culture of Bhaarath speaks of unity in diversity.

"Countries are many, but earth is one;
Stars are many, but sky is one;
Jewels are many, but gold is one;
Cows are many, but milk is one."

This is the spirit of unity that the culture of Bhaarath propagated since ancient times. You should give up worldly feelings and worldly thoughts and develop full faith in the principle of unity.

Embodiments of Love!

On this sacred day of Vijaya Dhashami take an oath to give up vices such as smoking, drinking and partaking of non-vegetarian food. Many do not realise the evil effects of these bad habits. If a smoker blows air on a white handkerchief, he will find yellow spots on it. This is a sign of disease. Smoking leads to cancer. Drinking is a demonic quality. It makes you intoxicated and to forget yourself. Consuming non-vegetarian food is also a bad quality. When human body itself is made of flesh, where is the need to consume the flesh of birds and animals? You should partake of only sacred food. Only then you will have sacred feelings. For sacred thoughts and sacred deeds, sacred food is essential. Even a noble soul like Bheeshma suffered on account of unsacred food. As a consequence, he had to lie on a bed of arrows for 56 days.

In order to have sacred feelings, apart from partaking of sacred food, you also need to have sacred vision. Do not cast bad looks on anybody. Do not speak ill of others. Do not hear anything that is bad. Do not entertain bad thoughts. Do not indulge in bad deeds. Do not hurt anybody. More than this there is nothing else one needs to do to improve one self.

HELP EVER; HURT NEVER

Human life is highly sacred. *"Janthoonaam Narajanma Dhurlabham"*, human birth is the rarest of all. But today some people kill fellow human beings without compassion. That is a demonic quality, not a human quality. Having taken human birth, you should not become a demon. In your old age when your vision is blurred and you cannot see properly, when your body becomes weak and decrepit, when everyone calls you old monkey, what is the use of repenting then? Undertake good actions from this moment.

Let everybody be happy. Do not harm anybody. Sage Vyaasa conveyed the essence of 18 puraanas in two sentences.

"Ashtaadasha Puraaneshu Vyaasasya Vachanadhvayam Paropakarah Punyaaya paapaaya Parapeedanam",

which means **"Help ever; Hurt never."** Do not hurt even an insect, because there is God in every creature. Basing on this, Saint Thyaagaraaja composed a song, in which he says, "O Raama, you are present in an ant and in Brahma."

NEVER BLAME GOD

Even such a great devotee like Thyaagaraaja began blaming Raama in times of difficulties. He said, "O Raama, don't you have the power to protect me, or do I lack devotion? Each and every hair of my body is filled with Your name. I am all the time thinking of You. So, certainly there is devotion in me. But you don't have the power." Immediately he sat in meditation and enquired within. He realised his mistake. Then he composed a song in which he said, "O Rama your power is so great and mighty, otherwise could a monkey like Hanumaan cross the ocean? Would Lakshmana who is Aadhisesha himself worship You? Would Lakshmi Devi, the Goddess of Wealth serve You? Would the most intelligent Bharatha obey Your command? Out of my foolishness I started blaming, forgetting Your Divinity. Please forgive me."

SEARCH FOR YOUR OWN FAULTS

When Jesus was being crucified, he cried out to God, "O God, why do You punish me like this?" Immediately he realised the Truth and said, "O God, may Your will prevail. It is You who created me, sustained me and protected me. I will not act against Your will. It was a mistake on my part to blame You." When he recognised his mistake, an ethereal voice said, "All are one my dear son, Be alike to everyone." Once you recognise your mistake, Divinity manifests. Man today does not recognise his mistakes; instead he looks for mistakes in others. Do not be bothered about others' faults; search for your own and rectify them. Only then your life will be sanctified.

Embodiments of Love!

Most importantly, you should develop Love. It contains all the other human values such as Sathya, Dharma and Shaanthi. Whatever you do, do it with love. Your Heart is like a big tank, senses are like taps. Fill the Heart with the water of Love. Only then you can experience love through all the senses.

Today, you talk of human values, but you do not seem to practise them. That makes Me very sad. You have been listening to many of My teachings; can you not practice at least one? Instead of teaching others, teach yourself and put into practice. What is the use of reading the Vedhas and sacred texts without practising them? Will you be cured of your disease, by merely repeating the names of the medicines? Will merely repeating the names of delicious items appease your hunger? Likewise, mere repetition of the name of the Lord is not enough. You should engage yourself in His work.

PARTICIPATE IN GOD'S WORK

When Hanumaan met Vibheeshana in Lanka, the latter said, "O Hanumaan, how lucky you are? In spite of being a monkey by birth, Raama has kept you in His company, but I have not been blessed with such an opportunity, though I chant His name constantly." Then Hanumaan replied, "O Vibheeshana, mere repetition of the Lord's name is not enough, you should participate in His work. Only then, you can be a recipient of His grace." As soon as Vibheeshana heard these words, he crossed the ocean, and fell at Raama's feet seeking His refuge. In this respect

we can say that Vibheeshana is greater than
Bheeshma. Vibheeshana tried to put his brothers
on the right path, but ultimately left them, as
they did not pay heed to his good counsels;
whereas, Bheeshma did not even make an attempt
to counsel Kauravas and continued to live with
them, being fully aware of their evil designs.

GOD TAKES CARE OF HIS DEVOTEES

When Vibhishana sought Rama's refuge,
Sugriva, Jambavantha opposed saying, "Swami,
you should never believe these rakshasas. There
must be some ulterior motive behind this act
of Vibheeshana. So ask him to return to Lanka."
Then Raama replied, "Once someone says, 'I
am yours', whoever he may be, I will take care
of him. So I will not reject Vibheeshana." This
is a testimony to God's Love.

Once you say "I am yours", then live up
to it with strong faith. Thereafter God will take
care of you at all places, and under all circumstances. I expect and bless you so that you develop
strong faith, give up vices, join good company,
entertain sacred feelings and attain Divinity.

(Bhagavaan concluded His Divine discourse
with the Bhajan, *"Prema mudhita manase kaho
Raama Raama Raam ..."*)

✳ ✳ ✳

SRI SATHYA SAI BOOKS AND PUBLICATIONS TRUST
PRASHAANTHI NILAYAM

PIN 515 134, ANANTAPUR DISTRICT, ANDHRA PRADESH, INDIA
IMPORTER/EXPORTER CODE NO.0990001032
RESERVE BANK OF INDIA EXPORTER CODE NO.HS-20001198.

THE VAAHINI SERIES: (Books written by Bhagvan Sri Sathya Sai Baba)

Bhagavatha Vaahini (The story of the Glory of the Lord)	25.00
Dharma Vaahini (The Path of Virtue and Morality)	12.00
Dhyana Vaahini (The Practice of Meditation)	12.00
Geetha Vaahini (The Divine Gospel)	22.00
Jnana Vaahini (The Stream of Eternal Wisdom)	12.00
Leela Kaivalya Vaahini (The Cosmic Play of God)	12.50
Prashanthi Vaahini (The Supreme Bliss of Divine)	12.00
Prasnothara Vaahini (Answers to Spiritual Questions)	15.00
Prema Vaahini (The Stream of Divine Love)	20.00
Rama Katha Rasa Vaahini Part-I (The Sweet Story of Rama's Glory)	38.00
Rama Katha Rasa Vaahini Part-I I(The Sweet Story of Rama's Glory)	28.00
Sandeha Nivarini (Clearance of Spiritual Doubts)	20.00
Sathya Sai Vaahini (Spiritual Message of Sri Sathya sai)	26.00
Sutra Vaahini (Analytical Aphorism on Supreme Reality)	16.00
Upanishad Vaahini (Essence of Vedic Knowledge)	17.50
Vidya Vaahini (Flow of Spiritual Education)	15.00

SATHYA SAI SPEAKS SERIES: (Discourses by Bhagavan Sri.Sathya Sai Baba)
(Revised & Enlarged Editions)

Sathya Sai speaks Vol I Years 1953 to 1960	30.00
Sathya Sai speaks Vol II Years 1961to 1962	38.00
Sathya Sai speaks Vol III Year 1963	35.00
Sathya Sai speaks Vol IV Year 1964	34.50
Sathya Sai speaks Vol V Year 1965	43.00
Sathya Sai speaks Vol VI Year 1966	45.00
Sathya Sai speaks Vol VII Year 1967	47.00
Sathya Sai speaks Vol VIII Year 1968	26.00
Sathya Sai speaks Vol IX Year 1969	30.00
Sathya Sai speaks Vol X Year 1970	36.50
Sathya Sai speaks Vol XI Years 1971 to 1972	51.00
Sathya Sai speaks Vol XII Years 1973 to 1974	36.00
Sathya Sai speaks Vol XIII Years 1975 to 1977	35.00
Sathya Sai speaks Vol XIV Years 1978 to 1980	45.00
Sathya Sai speaks Vol XV Years 1981 to 1982	47.00
Sathya Sai speaks Vol XVI Year 1983	39.00
Sathya Sai speaks Vol XVII Year 1984	42.00
Sathya Sai speaks Vol XVIII Year 1985	40.00
Sathya Sai speaks Vol XIX Year 1986	44.00
Sathya Sai speaks Vol XX Year 1987	40.00
Sathya Sai speaks Vol XXI Year 1988	40.00
Sathya Sai speaks Vol XXII Year 1989	40.00
Sathya Sai speaks Vol XXIII Year 1990	55.00
Sathya Sai speaks Vol XXIV Year 1991	63.00
Sathya Sai Speaks Vol XXV Year 1992	49.00
Sathya Sai Speaks Vol XXVI Year 1993	49.00
Sathya Sai Speaks Vol XXVII Year 1994	40.00

Sathya Sai Speaks Vol XXVIII Year 1995	45.00
Sathya Sai Speaks Vol XXIX Year 1996	50.00

SATHYAM SIVAM SUNDARAM SERIES:
(Life Story of Bhagavan Sri Sathya Sai Baba)

Sathyam Sivam Sundaram Part I (Birth to 1962)	29.00
Sathyam Sivam Sundaram Part II (Years 1962 to 1968)	29.00
Sathyam Sivam Sundaram Part III (Years 1969 to 1972)	33.00
Sathyam Sivam Sundaram Part IV (Years 1973 to 1979)	27.00

SUMMER SHOWER SERIES: (Discourses on Indian Culture and
Spirituality by Bhagavan Sri Sathya Sai Baba)

Summer Showers in Brindavan 1972	15.50
Summer Showers in Brindavan 1973	15.50
Summer Showers in Brindavan 1974	16.00
Summer Showers on the Blue Mountains (Ooty) 1976	14.50
Summer Showers in Brindavan 1977	17.50
Summer Showers in Brindavan 1978	13.50
Summer Showers in Brindavan 1979	14.50
Summer Showers in Brindavan 1990	26.00
Summer Showers in Brindavan 1993	27.00
Summer Showers in Brindavan 1996	20.00
Summer Showers in Brindavan 1995	30.00

FOR SALE ONLY IN INDIA

Pathways to God	35.00
Transformation of the Heart - by Judy Warner	27.00
Reconnecting the Love Energy - by Phyllis Krystal	25.00
Taming the Monkey Mind - by Phyllis Krystal	30.00
Suggestions for Study Groups and Individuals use of the Ceiling on Desires Programme by Phyllis Krystal	10.00
Catholic Priest Meets Sai Baba - By Don Mario Mazzolini	52.00

CHILDREN'S BOOKS:

Chinna Katha-part I	34.00
Chinna Katha-part II	37.00
My Life is My Message	19.00
Stories for Children: Part I	27.00
Stories for Children: Part II	23.00

OUR OTHER PUBLICATIONS:

Africa for Sai Baba-Volume I - by Dare Ogunkolati	2.50
Baba The Breath of Sai - By Grace J.Mc Martin	50.00
Conversation with Bhagavan Sri Sathya Sai Baba by Dr.John S. Hislop	47.00
Finding God -by Charles Penn	62.00
Gems of Wisdom	55.00
A Recapitulation of Baba's Divine Teachings - by Grace J.Mc Martin	53.00
Seva: A flower At His Lotus Feet-by Grace J.Mc Martin	25.00
Spirituality and Health-by Dr.(Mrs.)Charanjit Ghooi	80.00
Vision of Sai - Part I by Rita Bruce	42.00
Dasara Discourses '98	20.00
Vision of Sai - Part II by Rita Bruce	44.00
Benedictory Addresses - (15 Convocation Discourses by Bhagavan as Chancellor from beginning upto 1996)	29.00

Bhaktodharaka Sathya Sai - by N.Lakshmi Devamma	25.00
Easwaramma The chosen mother	20.00
Education in Human values	25.00
Garland of 108 Precious Gems-(108 Holy Names of Bhagavan)	20.00
Journey to God - Part I- by Jagadeesan	52.00
Journey to God - Part II- by Jagadeesan	86.00
Journey to God - Part III- by Jagadeesan	75.00
Loving God - by N.Kasturi	55.00
Life is a Game Play It - by Joy Thomas	50.00
Life is a Challenge Meet It - by Joy Thomas	39.00
Life is Love Enjoy It - by Joy Thomas	38.00
Life is a Dream Realise It - by Joy Thomas	33.00
My Baba and I - by Dr.John S.Hislop	47.00
My Beloved - by Charles Penn	35.00
Namasmarana	10.00
One Single Stream of Love	41.00
Prasanthi Pathways to Peace	14.00
Saadhana - The Inward Path	30.00
Sai Baba - The Ultimate Experience - Phyllis Krystal	44.00
Sairam - by Faith & Charles Penn	31.00
Sai Baba - The Holy Man and Psychiatrist - by Dr.Samuel H.Sandweiss	55.00
Spirit and the Mind - by Dr.Samuel H.Sandweiss	42.00
Sathya Sai - The Eternal Charioteer	46.00
Sai Baba's Mahavakya on Leadership (Hard Bound)	65.00
-by Lieut.Gen(Retd)Dr.M.L.Chibber	
Sai Messages for you and Me-Volume-I by Lucas Ralli	26.00
Sai Messages for you and Me-Volume-II by Lucas Ralli	25.00
Sathya Sai Baba God Incarnate - by Victor Kanu	30.00
The Greatest Adventure - by Dr.K.V.N.Murthy	55.00
To my father - by Justice Padma Khastgir	24.00
Quiz on Bhagavatham	10.00
Quiz on Mahaabhaarat	10.00
Quiz on Raamaayana	10.00
Quiz on Bhagavat Geetha	.8.00
Quiz on Divine life of Bhagawan Sri Sathya Sai Baba	10.00
Sai Baba and You - Practical Spirituality - by Mark and Barbara Gardner	25.00
Seeking Divinity - By Dr.John S.Hislop	60.00
Uniqueness of Swami and His Teachings - by Dr.A.Adivi Reddy	52.00
Thoughts for the Day	40.00
Tenfold Path to Divinity	34.00
Divine Memories - by Diana Baskin	38.00
The Light of Love	20.00
Sai Echoes from Kodai Hills	26.00
Truth is Only One	35.00
Universal and Practical Teachings of Bhgavan Baba	28.00
Prashaanthi Nilayam - Information Booklet	15.00

INLAND/OVERSEAS BOOK ORDERS AND SUBSCRIPTION FOR MONTHLY MAGAZINE SANATHANA SARATHI

Books are despatched by Regd. Book Post only subject to availability. Indents and remittences within India should be received by Money Order/Indian Postal Order/Account Payee Cheques/ Bank Drafts.

REMITTANCE - Remittances from Overseas towards book Orders/Sanathana Sarathi Subscriptions (English and Telugu) can be sent by A/C payee Bank cheque/Demand Draft/ International Money Order in FOREIGN CURRENCY ONLY AND NOT IN INDIAN RUPEES. Sending Cash Currency is liable to be confiscated by Government.

All remittences should be in favour of the THE CONVENER, SRI SATHYA SAI BOOKS AND PUBLICATIONS TRUST, PRASANTHI NILAYAM, ANANTHAPUR DISTRICT, ANDHRA PRADESH, INDIA, PIN CODE - 515 134, payable at State Bank of India, Prashaanthi Nilayam (Branch Code No.2786) mentioning full address in capitals with Area Pin Code, Zip Code No., where the books are to be despatched.

POSTAGE (INLAND)

At the rate of 50 paise per 100 gms plus Registration charges Rs.10/-. For an order of 1kg parcel, postage Rs.5/- (+) Regn.charges Rs.10/-; total Rs.15/-. For 2 kgs parcel Rs.20/-; For 3 kgs parcels Rs.25/-; For 4 kgs parcel Rs.30/- and 5 kgs parcel Rs.35/-

While remitting, please calculate the cost of the books indented (+) postage (+) Registration charges.

POSTAGE (OVERSEAS)

1 kg Parcel Rs. 60.00
2 kg Parcel Rs. 78.00
3 kg Parcel Rs.110.00
4 kg Parcel Rs.140.00
5 kg Parcel Rs.172.00

(Packing and Forwarding charges Rs.20.00 extra)